PRO-
CRAS-
TIN-
ATOR'S

SUCCESS
KIT

Alyce Cornyn-Selby

BEYNCH·PRESS

Copyright© 1986 by Alyce P. Cornyn-Selby

Sixth Printing 1994

Also by Alyce P. Cornyn-Selby:
The Man Who Ran Out of Words
Take Your Hands Off My Attitude

Published by BEYNCH PRESS
1928 S.E. Ladd Avenue
Portland, Oregon 97214
503-232-0433

Printed in the United States of America. All rights reserved. No part of this publication may be reproduced in any form or by any means, photocopying or otherwise, without prior written permission.

Library of Congress Cataloging-in-Publication Data

Cornyn-Selby, Alyce, 1946-
Procrastinator's success kit.

1. Procrastination.   2. Self-actualization
(Psychology)   I. Title.
BF575.P95C67   1986   158'.1   86-33444
ISBN 0-941383-03-2

More Praise for the Procrastinator's Success Kit!

"Gentle humor and choices. Not once in this book did I feel I'd been banged over the head."

Ida Martyn (Portland, Oregon)

"A familiar litany of my style . . . the use of anecdotes and humor carried the day. I'm impressed!"

George Tate (Honolulu, Hawaii)

"Well-written and handsome."

Peter Renner (Vancouver, Canada)

"Provocative, entertaining, and best of all, useful!"

Robert Foster (Portland, Oregon)

"I opened the innocent-looking **Procrastinator's Success Kit**. My mouth fell open; I silently asked, "HOW did she KNOW?""

B.J. Borden (Austin, Texas)

"This is the **best** book published on the subject that I've ever seen!"

Jim Moran (Portland, Oregon)

"Useful and straightforward self-help book, refreshingly so!"

Jeanne Dockham (Vancouver, Washington)

Dedication
to T. Bearsa
This book would not have been possible without his inspiration and creativity.

Disciple: "*Master, why is there evil in the world?*"
Master: "*To thicken the plot.*"
Disciple: "*Then what is success?*"
Master: "*Did you get what you wanted?*"

TABLE OF CONTENTS

                                                            Page

1. HOW WOULD YOUR LIFE BE DIFFERENT IF YOU DIDN'T PUT THINGS OFF?............1

    The Equalizer/Diversion/The 8 Key Questions/ Put-It-Off Audit/Honesty & Benefits/First Aid

2. SELF-SABOTAGE: YOUR SURVIVAL MECHANISMS AT WORK....................23

    General Nature of Self-Sabotage/Miracle of the Brown Volvo/Jim's Story/The Teenager & the Fur Coat/Who *Are* These People?/ How to Talk to Them/Hey, Show A Little Respect/The Journal/The Weight Sabotage

3. PROCRASTINATION AS A CREATIVE ACT...65

    What's So Creative About Procrastination?/ The Successful Procrastinator/Agony & Guilt/ The Eight Procrastinating Styles:

    The Little Bo Peep & the Back Burner Procrastinator....................................80
    The Action Junkie Procrastinator................95
    The Rebellious Procrastinator...................108
    The Perfectionist Procrastinator................120
    The Crazymaking Procrastinator................141
    The "Nice" Procrastinator......................162
    The "Don't Rely on Me!" Procrastinator........174
    The Feeling Good Procrastinator...............184

    Each section includes: Title and Description
                                      Pay Values
                                      Prescriptions
                                      Identifying Self-Talk
                                      Wall Mottos
                                      Combat Tactics

4. WHAT ARE MY OPTIONS?..................195

ABOUT THE AUTHOR

Alyce P. Cornyn-Selby is a human being and, therefore, by definition, procrastinates.

But she didn't procrastinate much on this book.

Alyce   Alyce   Alyce

In 1985, Alyce developed "GOAL CALL," the only trademarked system for dealing with procrastination and called "The greatest anti-procrastination device available."

GOAL CALL has been featured on the front page of the *Daily Journal of Commerce* (with a rather nice picture of our Alyce) and Northwest Airlines in-flight magazine reviewed GOAL CALL for high flying procrastinators. USA Cable Network television, CBS News, KATU-ABC, newspapers and radio have interviewed Alyce about her unusual approach to the age-old problem of putting things off.

An informative and entertaining speaker, Alyce's approach to "cracking communication" codes ranges from marketing strategies to intrapersonal communciation (self-talk). A corporate manager for 12 years, Alyce now lectures on management and communciation issues for colleges, business and government.

Alyce was recently named to Britain's *Foremost Women of the Twentieth Century* for her contribution to education and communication. Also: *Who's Who in America, Who's Who in Colleges & Universities, Who's Who in the West, Who's Who in Finance & Industry,* and *Who's Who of International Women*.
   —Travis Duncan

INTRODUCTION...

There is a benefit to procrastinating...
to add a little drama to life,
to drive people away,
or to be rescued...many reasons, many benefits.

For one reason or another,
we procrastinate because we need to
in order to get what we want.

So it's very dangerous to consider
NOT PROCRASTINATING.

Consider what you get from procrastinating
and deal with that.

Maybe you can get what you want out of life
and not procrastinate
but maybe not.

What do I get from procrastinating?
And do I want to change it?
Maybe.

Consider the options.

CHAPTER 1
HOW WOULD YOUR LIFE BE DIFFERENT IF YOU DIDN'T PUT THINGS OFF?

Have you ever ruined a career or a marriage due to procrastination? Some people have.

Have you ever put your health in jeopardy by putting off seeing a doctor or "forgetting" to take medication? Many people have.

Have you ever promised yourself that *someday* you'll take that dream trip...or *someday* you'll write that letter? Most of us have.

Have you planned diets and exercise programs, started a journal, intended to take a class, wanted to read *War and Peace*?

Procrastination.

The one universal equalizer. We all do it. We all talk to ourselves about it and then do it ANYWAY.

Procrastination does not discriminate and it's extremely versatile. It affects men and women equally and every race and religion. It is cross cultural. It is also portable, compact, has no moving parts, requires no training, one size seems to fit all and it can be literally hazardous to your health.

It's also creative.

In fact, people are never more creative than when they're sabotaging their own efforts...and often never more *productive* than when they are *procrastinating*.

"Oh, sure!" said the executive director for a West Coast port authority. "My house was never in better repair than when I was working on my Ph.D.!"

Procrastinating — and avoiding one task — means that we will fill up our time with other tasks. Sometimes they are important tasks and sometimes they're not...

For me, it's taxes.

I will find any diversion to keep me from completing my tax return. Sometimes the diversion is so uncharacteristic of my usual behavior that it becomes obvious to family members. You see, my domestic sense is about as developed as an Oregon swamp. So when my daughter watched me *polishing the silverware* no less, she asked (knowingly), "Oh...tax time?"

The simple fact of the matter is: while we're racing 90 m.p.h. *away* from a goal we've set for ourselves, WE ARE NOT ASLEEP. We are active, organized and *creative*.

"I put off working on the annual report until the last two weeks," explained the graphic designer. "Then everybody leaves me alone — it's a top priority — and all I have to do is look rushed and say, 'Sorry, I've got the annual report' and people treat me like I'm special...they leave me alone."

Procrastination becomes an efficient communication device for dealing with other people. A perfect method for adding drama to life is to wait until the deadline looms large.

Although the human talent lost to procrastination is incalculable — thousands of college degrees started and never finished, pages of letters half-written, business start ups and melt downs, weight lost and gained and lost and gained, scores of garages and attics never cleaned — procrastination is also responsible for splendid ideas, unusual hobbies, successful retail sales (I know *I'd* rather go shopping than just about anything!), high TV ratings, fresh perspectives, missed opportunities that were better off missed and, of course, polished silverware.

This book will answer the following questions:
1. What is procrastination?
2. Why do people do it?
3. Why do *I* do it?
4. When am I going to get things done?
5. What's so creative about procrastination?
6. What if I hate goal setting?
7. How can I find the time to read this book?
8. How can I get myself to do ANYTHING?

Getting to know your own procrastination is a real, practical, down-to-the-heart-of-it knowing your Self. And as a procrastinator, you are a human being at your most creative, your most bizarre and your most human moment. The ultimate knowing of yourself is knowing your own procrastination.

Procrastination becomes serious business when it's hazardous to your health — the medical check up you put off, the medication that you "forgot" to take, the exercise program that lasted a week. Self-management of procrastination behavior becomes critical under some circumstances. There will be plenty of tips and tools in this book for creating practical, interesting and personalized solutions to procrastination.

Phone calls go unanswered, subscriptions slip, wills go unwritten, warrantees run out, oil goes unchanged in the car and exercise machines gather dust. And yet, while you are avoiding paying your bills — by walking the dog, organizing your sock drawer, calling a friend or dusting the top of the refrigerator — you are busy. Meanwhile, your friend who is putting off walking his dog, is doing what? Paying his bills.

For instance...

How do you finally get around to writing a book?

I enjoy a certain "expert" standing among procrastinators. I developed the only trademarked system for dealing with procrastination. It's called Goal Call and it is a service offered through my consulting firm. I speak nationwide on the subject of self-sabotage and creative procrastination for colleges, government agencies and private industry. National cable television interviewed me about this mysterious human trait and the *Daily Journal of Commerce* devoted a front page story to its possible solution. Procrastinators from around the country wrote to me when an in-flight magazine published an article about my ideas.

So I've got it aced, right? Wrong!

I may be a lot of things, but I am, first and foremost: A HUMAN BEING. And I call procrastination — the fascinating art of being human. I'd lose my badge that says "human" if I didn't procrastinate about *something*.

So how did I finally get around to writing this book?

Simple.
It's tax time.

THE PUT-IT-OFF AUDIT

I'd rather clean an oven than do my taxes. You'd rather pay bills than clean an oven. I'd rather walk the dog than wash the car. You'd rather write Mom than walk the dog. Everybody has their own areas of procrastination. Remember, "show me what you avoid and I will show you your internal genius."

So here is a structure that will allow you to know yourself a little better. We generally procrastinate in the following areas: maintenance of stuff, maintenance of me, maintenance of relationships, paperwork of life, commerce (employment or our own business), education and personal enrichment or planning.

Do you save all your procrastinating for home life? (Gee, how fortunate for your co-workers...) Do you just procrastinate on personal matters? Do you take perfect care of your friends and co-workers and imperfect care of yourself? Do you only postpone creative things? Or pleasant, recreational activities? Where does money figure into your procrastinating? Do you cash your check the day you receive it and then put off purchases? If you run your own business, do you drag your feet about sending out the invoices? Or is it just taxes?

HOW TO USE THE PUT-IT-OFF AUDIT

Take only one minute with each audit. There are seven audits. The purpose of the audit is *not* to create a grievance list of your past offenses. Go through the items rapidly to get your initial reactions...these are what will give you the most important information about your patterns. Remember, just one minute per audit.

You may find it helpful to mark the item (y) yes, (n) no, or (s) sometimes.

Maintenance of Stuff

_____ Grocery shopping

_____ Putting things away

_____ Food preparation

_____ Showing up to eat on time

_____ Kitchen clean up

_____ The Yard

_____ The garage, shop or attic

_____ Vehicle upkeep, warrantee checks, oil, tires, etc.

_____ Getting broken things fixed

_____ Pets: vaccinations, feeding, exercising, etc.

_____ Selling unwanted or unused articles

_____ Donating unwanted and unused articles

_____ Taking the bottles back (or newspapers, etc.)

_____ Large, major projects like sanding floors, painting the exterior, rebuilding the porch, adding a room

Maintenance of Me

_____ Vitamins every day

_____ Regularly watch the weight

_____ Regular medical check ups

_____ Regular dental check ups

_____ Out-of-the-ordinary care (medical)

_____ Out-of-the-ordinary care (dental)

_____ Regular exercise

_____ Personal little stuff (filing your nails, brushing your teeth, shaving, etc.)

_____ Making appointments for hair care, cosmetic attention

_____ Finding a new barber or beautician when the usual one is missing or incompetent

_____ Getting glasses or dentures

_____ Getting glasses or dentures repaired

_____ Maintenance of clothes and shoes

_____ Keeping a journal

_____ Donating blood

Maintenance of Relationships

_____ Remember birthdays
_____ Remember appropriate holidays (Valentine's Day)
_____ Remember anniversaries
_____ Send sympathy messages when appropriate
_____ Send congratulations when appropriate
_____ Show up on time
_____ Return telephone calls
_____ Return lunch and/or dinner invitation
_____ Compliment freely and often
_____ Returning letters...writing back
_____ Asking a question
_____ Asking for help
_____ Networking for information
_____ Being honest; saying "no"
_____ Keeping a confidence
_____ Remembering important events about this person
_____ Planning events (movies, sports, trips) with friends
_____ Offering help
_____ Being away from home and sending a post card

Paperwork of Life

_____ Will

_____ Insurance

_____ Estate planning

_____ Financial planning

_____ Saving warrantees

_____ Clipping coupons and actually using them

_____ Sending in the rebate

_____ Paying bills

_____ Doing your taxes

_____ Hiring an accountant

_____ Renewing licenses

_____ Paying parking tickets

_____ Balancing checkbook

_____ Paying back a loan

_____ Library fines and returning books

_____ Funeral plans

_____ Subscriptions

_____ Record or book club monthly cards

_____ Donations to favorite charities

_____ Personal files in order

_____ Safety deposit box

Commerce

_____ Performance appraisal

_____ Monthly report

_____ Weekly report

_____ Getting to work place on time

_____ Finding work

_____ Doing reports

_____ Returning business calls

_____ "Forgetting" about meetings

_____ Deadending projects

_____ Invoicing clients or customers

_____ Doing your business plan

_____ Doing your financial plan

_____ Learning something new (how to run computer, etc.)

_____ Writing a complimentary note or letter

_____ Writing a reference

_____ Hiring a new person

_____ Giving a presentation

_____ Calling your boss

_____ Critique of a peer's work

_____ Reprimanding an employee

_____ Praising an employee

_____ Signing approval on purchase orders, financial papers

Education

_____ Signing up for a class
_____ Applying for additional coursework
_____ Requesting transcripts
_____ Getting to class on time
_____ Preparing for class presentation
_____ Preparing for class test
_____ Preparing for class discussion
_____ Doing research
_____ Reading
_____ Writing
_____ Completing requirements
_____ Filling out forms
_____ Getting additional instruction
_____ Asking for explanation
_____ Signing up for adult education class (Fun-type, like acting, etc.)

Personal enrichment or planning

_____ Your 5-year plan
_____ Your 10-year plan
_____ Your 20-year plan
_____ Retirement plans
_____ Reading self-help book
_____ Keeping a journal
_____ Seeing a counselor to work on specific problem
_____ Taking time to smell the roses
_____ Planned weekly activity done alone
_____ Cultural (music, plays, movies)
_____ Learning to play a musical instrument
_____ Writing
_____ Visual arts (painting, photography, etc.)
_____ Talking over a situation with a friend
_____ Learning a foreign language

Now take as much time as you need to analyze your responses. You'll be looking for the common denominators to your procrastination.

Notice any similarities in the activities that you have checked? Do they all involve paper? Or physical activity? Or decisions? Or money?

You may have indicated that you procrastinate about the yardwork...maybe cutting the grass. And you know that you could have the neighbor kid do it for a small price. What prevents you from hiring the unpleasant task done?

How big a deal is it? Is your procrastinating a problem for just you? Are there others that are affected by your procrastinating? Do you let the lawn grow until the neighbors complain to the city? Or does it just bother you when the grass gets about 2-1/2 inches high?

If you like to have your life "squared away" on the financial level, the physical level, the emotional level, relationship-wise, work-wise and have everything properly maintained, then get realistic. It's never done. As one car buff said about his antique masterpiece: "You start at one end and work to the other end. And when you get there...you just start over."

Dirty dishes in the sink are not punishable by imprisonment. A dirty pan soaking in the sink might be OK during tax time, for instance. Give yourself a break. Lighten up.

What Do You Do Instead?

_____ Read the newspaper
_____ Read catalogues
_____ Read trashy magazines/books
_____ Take a bath
_____ Eat
_____ Exercise
_____ "Shop 'Til You Drop"
_____ Watch TV
_____ Talk on the telephone
_____ Sleep
_____ Complain to anyone who will listen
_____ Leave, go to the movies
_____ Play video games
_____ Take drugs, sleeping pills
_____ Drink
_____ Go for a drive
_____ Clean

FIRST AID

Aid #1: Are you dressed for the part?

Jean was a corporate manager who had gotten into management without the benefit of a degree. When she went back to college to finish (at the age of 32) she found, to her dismay, that she procrastinated about her assignments. "I never procrastinate about my work," she explained. Then one weekend, Jean discovered an interesting aspect to her school work. "I discovered that if I dressed like a college kid, I could somehow study and write easier. I wore an old blue jean skirt and a sweatshirt and 'played the part' — the next thing I knew, I wasn't just pretending to be a college student, I was being a college student."

Jean discovered the Power of the Costume. Do you need to discover it too? If you hate gardening and your Aunt Tillie loved gardening and she always wore a straw hat, then go buy a straw hat. It sounds nuts...and it works.

Aid #2:   Give it a try.

Agree to do it poorly and not very creatively; just take a stab at it. Do something that you'll hide later. Nobody will see it but you. If you had only 30 seconds to get it done, what would you do next?

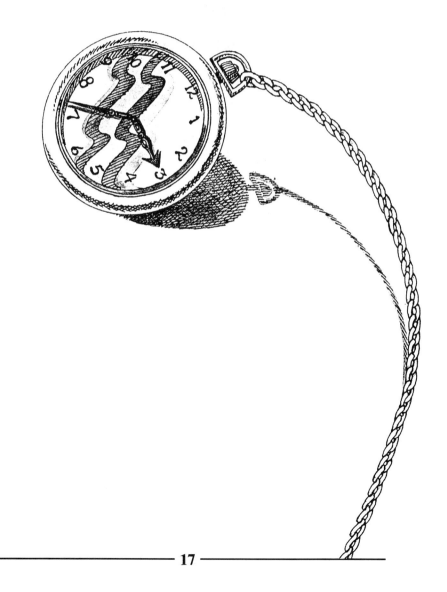

Aid #3: Chunk it down.

There is no problem too small but what it can't be made even smaller. If you're going to write a letter, just go find a stamp. That's all. Don't allow yourself to do anything more. Then this evening, find the paper and a pen. Don't do *one more thing*! Tomorrow start the letter and only allow yourself five minutes with it.

Chunking down a problem is like sex therapy. The therapist prescribes foreplay but no real interaction. The pressure is off. This works with procrastination... when you'd like to get on with your life and your tasks. If you have a task that you really, really want to work on, chunk it down into the tiniest bits that you can and only allow yourself to do a piece at a time.

Aid #4: Imagine that the task is finished and that there are terrible repercussions as a result.

You finally got around to washing the dog and the animal now has pneumonia. Or you got your taxes finished early and surprised the IRS who now insist on an audit. Or you prepared for your presentation and went whole-hog on expensive slides only to have the thing cancelled and your boss is furious because you spent the money...

What's the worst that could happen? You might just as well get it out and talk about it because there is a person on the inside of you that suspects this scene anyway.

Aid #5: What would happen if you got passionate about this task?

If your procrastinated task is to clean the garage, what would happen if you walked out there whistling, playing Tina Turner on a boom box and started in on it with great gusto? Would the rest of the family think that you've lost your mind? Why are you so afraid of looking like a nut?

What would happen if your compulsion to avoid this task was suddenly turned into a compulsion to finish the task? Imagine what that would be like. In vivid detail. What do you look like when you're enthusiastic? (The word "enthusiasm" comes from the Greek meaning "The God within you.")

What if you got passionate about writing that book? Gosh, everybody would know about it and they'd know when it didn't get published, wouldn't they? So what. If you're thinking about creating an invention, create it. What if it fails? Thomas J. Watson, the founder of IBM, said: "The way to succeed is to double your failure rate." So design it! Compose it! Write it! Paint it! Risk it! Call him! Call her! People who are passionate are *irresistible* people.

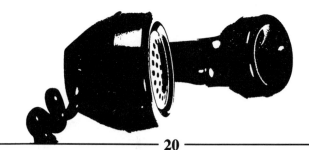

THE MAJOR QUESTION

How would things be different if you did not procrastinate? That is, if you never put anything off, what would your life look like?

First, this would happen... _____

_____

_____

I'd probably have no... _____

_____

_____

_____

As long as I can keep procrastinating, I... _____

_____

_____

_____

Procrastinating isn't so bad compared to, say... _____

_____

_____

_____

_____

If I could stop procrastinating, I could probably... _____

_____

_____

_____

(From Alyce's Journal...)

If I never put anything off, what would my life look like?

"No fun.

No sleep.

I'd be so organized and disciplined that there would be no room for spontaneity or happy 'mistakes' or chats at La Patisserie or Sunday drives down the Columbia Gorge.

If I never put things off, then life would get awfully predictable, wouldn't it?

Or would it?

Would I still be human?"

CHAPTER 2
SELF-SABOTAGE:
THE FASCINATING ART OF BEING HUMAN

Life didn't make much sense to me until I studied sabotage.

Not the kind of sabotage that involves blowing up military installations or diverting freight trains. I mean the kind of sabotage that human beings perform on themselves: self-sabotage.

My interest in self-sabotage came from my research for a University of Hawaii course on employee performance appraisals. A key element in that research was: what motivates people to work?

What motivates a person to do anything? What motivates you?

To understand human behavior (which didn't make a lot of sense to me, including my own behavior), I began to find information on why people *don't do* what they say they want to do. Why would we do that? Why would we say we wanted something and then not do it? For whatever reasons, we all have this in common. It became, to me, the fascinating art of being human. And procrastination is our hands-down favorite form of sabotaging ourselves.

The dictionary defines "sabotage" as:
1. deliberate subversion.
2. an act tending to hamper or hurt.

The definition of Self-Sabotage, then, is: WHEN WE SAY WE'RE GOING TO DO SOMETHING AND THEN WE GO ABOUT MAKING SURE THAT IT DOESN'T HAPPEN.

Self-sabotage has some unique characteristics. First, it is almost totally a human activity. I don't think that dogs procrastinate, for instance. Your pup doesn't look across the street at a cat and say, "Ahhh, I think I'll go bite that cat next Tuesday." No. They get up and go bite the cat.

Secondly, it appears to be something that we develop, maybe even something that we learn. For instance, small children do not put off asking for a cookie. They don't seem to ponder questions like "Do I deserve it?" "Would I be bothering anyone by asking?" or "Perhaps later would be a better time." No. Instead, they say, "Cookie, NOW!"

Thirdly, the person doing the sabotage is the one least likely to recognize it. Rarely do we notice that we're sabotaging our efforts. It is pretty simple for us to recognize it in others, however.

An example: The best place to listen to people talking about diets and losing weight is to eavesdrop in a restaurant or ice cream parlor. The Weight Sabotage is one of the easiest to identify because we're actually wearing the results around our middles. It is fascinating to me to hear two people discussing the merits of Weight Loss Clinic versus Diet Center while polishing off a second helping of German Chocolate cake. I encourage you to witness this phenomenon for yourself the next time you're out dining.

Most self-sabotage is not easily recognizable.

Here are a few forms of what might be called self-sabotage:
- accidents
- procrastination
- losing weight and gaining weight and losing weight and gaining weight and losing weight
- a string of "relationships"
- a string of jobs
- something that appears on your "to do" list more than 10 times
- hearing yourself make commitments and then watching yourself not keep them
- habitual lateness
- "forgetfulness"
- setting up a plan and then not doing it

And some common things that get sabotaged:
- weight loss program
- exercise program
- VISA or Mastercard
- "I'm going to write a novel someday"
- taxes or financial planning in general
- cleaning out the garage, attic, closet or back of your car
- writing thank you notes

In order to understand procrastination, we need to have a foundation of understanding of how self-sabotage works. Two stories illustrate self-sabotage well and after reading them, you will be an expert. Keep in mind, that everyone is being touched by sabotage...and it can be:

someone you work with,

someone you live with,

or you.

The Miracle of the Brown Volvo

You have this brown Volvo and one day you park it in the grocery store parking lot and someone opens their door into the side of your car. A few weeks later you lose the car's antenna in the automatic car wash. Then you scrape the chrome bumper downtown in an unusually tricky angle parking space. And somehow or other the car goes by its 3,000 mile check and then its 5,000 mile check. No one really mentions it, so you don't bother to have the oil changed. Then one day a friend of yours with a history of drinking problems asks if he can use your Volvo to drive to the airport...and you hand over the keys.

Now, any one of these events BY ITSELF probably doesn't mean much.

Next, you're on your way out to the Volvo with a business associate who looks at the car and says to you, "Gee, when are you going to get a new car?"

That does it! You go down to the dealership and check out that red sports car that you've been seeing in the showroom window for the last few months. You trade in the Volvo and as you get into the little red car, you say to yourself, "Ah, this is more like *me*!"

At no time were you aware that you were sabotaging your brown Volvo. You won't recognize your own sabotaging for this reason: in between those incidents with the Volvo were several thousand *other* incidents in your life. Until the little mishaps and forgetful times are stacked up together in one paragraph, you can't see what is going on with the Volvo. And many of the facts were so insignificant that they weren't worth remembering. But they are signposts to people who are outside of you.

We all have brown Volvos in our lives. At any time of the day or night or any time of year you have something in your life that is your brown Volvo. Or you may have several of them going at once. That's not unusual.

Why can't we just simply bag the brown Volvos in our lives? Well, in this story we all know that Volvo makes a car to last and it will with proper care. To simply get rid of it might raise the question, "What's *wrong* with it?" Instead, we wait until it *looks* bad enough... and then we get rid of it.

Examples:

If George moves from one apartment into another apartment, his friend Harold asks, "What was wrong with the old apartment?" If Jeannie closes her bank accounts and starts banking at a different place, her co-worker asks, "What was wrong with the old bank?"

And then there is the ever popular American past-time of "What's wrong with the old spouse?"... only you're expected to beat everyone to the punch and *tell* them what is wrong with him or her before they even ask the question. We *tell* to get permission (from ourselves, actually) to leave or move or divorce or whatever. If the argument sounds good enough to us, we may go through with it.

But sometimes the Volvo has to get pretty well beaten up before we will finally trade it in.

The second sabotage story is not a symbolic story; it is a true story.

Jim's Story

Several years ago when I was a manager in a corporation, I had a position open in my department. We advertised and read resumes and interviewed people, but the supervisor of the department and I could not find anyone with the specialized skills that we wanted. So we advertised in the Seattle papers and found someone to fit the bill. Jim.

We moved Jim and his wife and two children to Portland. Everything went well for two years. Then, for some strange reason, Jim began to take issue with things. The relationships with people in other departments were the first to get Jim's ire. Soon it was other people in his own work area that felt the effect. Two months went by and Jim's supervisor was having no luck altering Jim's behavior or lightening Jim's daily black moods. The three of us had several boardroom chats and talking with Jim was like trying to make pleasant conversation with a hemorrhoidal pit bull.

Jim's supervisor, a sensitive and effective management-type, was saddened that Jim was not happy. I wasn't too happy either. Things got worse. Jim's supervisor and I began to take Jim's behavior personally.

I had been keeping my boss, a vice-president, informed about this personnel problem. An astute observer of human behavior, my boss said: "It looks like Jim is trying to get fired."

AH! Ah-ha! A light went on! It had never occurred to me that anyone would actually *try* to be fired! That didn't make sense to me...until my boss suggested it.

After another week of trying to pretend that there wasn't a problem, we began to deal with it. We gave Jim two options: either go to out-placement counseling which essentially gets the employee out of the company, or go to a career counselor/psychotherapist. Jim chose therapy and after three sessions, the change was noticeable.

I could hardly believe it. After months of growling, Jim was coming to work with a smile on his face. I was sure that the therapist must have performed brain surgery on Jim because nothing had changed in Jim's work environment. Jim's supervisor was relieved. I was elated. Harmony was restored. What on earth had happened?

Well, it didn't have anything to do with me or with Jim's supervisor. (We needn't have taken it personally after all.) It went like this...

Jim was married and lived with his security-oriented wife and their two children. If Jim had come home from work and said, "I quit," his wife would have killed him. BUT, if he came home and said, "I got fired," she would have said, "Oh, poor Jim, we'll make it. We'll go back home to Seattle and work things out."

And, you see, that's what Jim wanted all along. What he really wanted deep down inside was to go back to Seattle. He wasn't consciously aware of that, however. He could have passed a lie detector test saying he wanted to work for us. But something on the inside of Jim wanted to go back to Seattle badly enough to get him fired over it.

Jim wasn't dishonest. He was no more aware of his deep, inner drives than you are of that slight pressure in your shoulders right now. There is a lot going on that we're not perfectly aware of every single day.

There was no way that Jim's supervisor and I could have turned Portland, Oregon into Seattle, Washington. Once Jim's desires were known, however, the supervisor helped Jim find another job...in Seattle. The family moved after we had a little going-away party and Jim sent us postcards.

This story almost had an unhappy ending. We nearly fired Jim...that would have been uncomfortable for Jim but also very upsetting for us. Instead, we did what I call "living life gracefully"...finding the sabotage and doing something constructive about it.

Are you beginning to see how self-sabotage works?

OK, *now what to do?*

Have you ever said to yourself: "There's somebody on the inside of me who..."? Or have you ever said, "Well, part of me wants to...but part of me doesn't"?

If you have, then you're 90% home free on solving a sabotage problem.

YOU MAY BE UNKNOWINGLY SABOTAGING YOUR WORK.

OR SOMEONE YOU WORK WITH MAY BE SABOTAGING THEIR WORK.

(Think about it...are you an innocent bystander to someone else's sabotage?)

OR SOMEONE YOU KNOW MAY BE SABOTAGING THEIR PERSONAL RELATIONSHIP.

(Think about it...are you an innocent bystander to someone else's sabotage? Are you "unknowingly" sabotaging your personal relationships?)

SELF-SABOTAGE IS WHEN THERE IS A DISPARITY BETWEEN OUR WORDS AND OUR ACTIONS.

The Teenager and the Fur Coat Story

Have you made a large purchase recently? I don't mean in size, I mean in cost. Have you bought a house or a car or a boat or a piece of jewelry that set you back a few coins? How did you buy it? Did you just see it and lay the money down? Or was there a conversation inside of yourself about it?

For this next example, we are going to listen in on the inner conversation of a teenage girl who is home from college for the holidays. She is shopping and she has just discovered a white rabbit coat. If you could tune in, you would hear...

"Oh, it's BEAUTIFUL." (Hands reach for the soft fur and pull the sleeve out for a better look. A large red tag screams the price. Frown.)

"Ooooo, costs so much..."

Then. "Ah, but I would look so good on the ski slopes in this coat..."

"But it's so much money. If you get this coat, there won't be enough money left to GET ON THE SLOPES!"

Then..."It's made out of fur...it's durable and it will keep me warm."

Then..."It's white, it'll get dirty fast."

Then..."Oh, what would my friends think...me wearing real fur. An animal had to die for this coat."

And the last voice says, "THUMPER!"

In the span of a few seconds, this teenager has experienced six different characters within her...all voicing their opinions and attempting to influence the purchase or the passing up of this rabbit coat. Who are these voices and what is their mission?

Let's look at the conversation again:

"Oh, it's beautiful" and "I would look so good in this coat" is spoken by the internal **P.R. Director** (P.R., as in Public Relations.) The internal P.R. Director is responsible for keeping you looking "hip, slick and cool." Your P.R. Director dressed you this morning. Your P.R. Director is probably the one who wanted that red sports car. Your internal P.R. Director is the one who is mortified when your friend tells you that you've had a piece of spinach between your teeth all afternoon. Your P.R. Director is the one who says, "Well, better send a Christmas card to them since they sent one to us."

The internal P.R. Director is an extremely important person in our inner scheme of things. We would make life uncomfortable for ourselves and for others without this internal guide.

Okay, who said, "Ooooo, it's too much money"?

That's the **Financial Director.**

Now you probably know people who have an internal Financial Director who is either asleep or on drugs or is just simply *not there*. These are people who have never balanced a checkbook, never will and have no guilt or desire in that area. They may push their VISA or MasterCard up over its limits several times a year, "forget" to pay their bills, always get an extension on their taxes and may even misplace their money. Their internal Financial Director is just not a very influential person.

That's not the case with most people. When I talk about the Director of Finance, I am reminded to tell you that not all these internal voices have equal say. This is not a democracy. And for many of us, the Financial Director has the final say in most decisions...a powerful personality. You cannot get up and walk across the room until the Financial Director says it's okay.

Sometimes we are so controlled by the Financial Director that we may go on a buying binge just to see if we still know how to say, "Charge it!" Frequently I will hear someone tell a story of how they pinched pennies for months and then suddenly dropped a big load of dollars on a luxury item. And it felt good. This should tell you that internal power plays are going on constantly.

Okay, back to the teenager with the coat. Who said, "It's white, it'll get dirty fast"? Most people call that voice their **Internal Mom**. Did *anybody* have a mother who said, "It's white. Buy it! It'll look great on you!"?

Okay, who said, "It's durable, it'll keep me warm"? Most, but not all, call this the **Internal Dad**. Both have a streak of "let's be practical" about their opinions.

Okay, who said, "What will my friends think"? That's the **Social Conscience** speaking. The internal Social Conscience is the person who tries to keep the relationship with you and the mass mind in synch. Your Social Conscience won't let you throw trash out of your car window anymore. Maybe your Social Conscience is the one who convinced you to stop smoking. Your Social Conscience will get you into the voting booth on election day and maybe convince you to work for a political cause. Depending on the power you give your Social Conscience, you may even run for public office. In the case of the teenager, she is concerned that the wearing of fur will not set too kindly with her friends who oppose the killing of animals for coat purposes.

And, finally, who said, "THUMPER!"? That's the **Internal Child**. This internal person relates to your environment the way that you did when you were a little person.

Exercise: What is your age? Take that number and multiply it by 365 days. Not including a few leap years, if you're 40 years old, you've been on this planet 14,600 days...more or less. And you have been a different YOU every one of those 14,600 days. You've learned something every day whether you wanted to or not. Some of the things you've learned, you didn't want to know, but you learned anyway.

So if you are 40 years old, there are really 14,600 of you all walking around in one person. And each one of those 14,600 people has a voice. And chances are they talk to you.

I have a friend who says, "Yeah, I know what that's like. I wake up in the morning, the jury is in and I'M GUILTY!"

Here other internal characters common to most of us...

There's the **Health Director**. This person is responsible for getting you to the doctor when you need to go. This person is the influence in your life that makes you take your vitamins, fasten your seatbelt and brush your teeth. The Health Director has your physical survival in mind. That's *their* priority and that's their mission.

The **Time Keeper**. For some of us, this is the ulcer producer. The Time Keeper insists that we be punctual to every event, meeting, appointment, movie, game or social gathering. Eight o'clock does *not* mean 8:01 to a good Time Keeper. However, the Time Keeper is the one who makes you leave your fingerprints in the steering wheel of your car when you're stuck in traffic and late for an appointment. God forbid that you should ever arrive late.

On the other hand, some people have Time Keepers who are a bit lax. Being late is not a felony. And 8:00 means really maybe 9:00.

Another internal character is the **Clean Freak**. Somewhere inside of you is a person who tolerates just a certain level of mess in your environment. You might even call this person your Internal Environmental Protection Agency.

The *Odd Couple* is the classical example of two people with two very different internal Clean Freaks. The slob can withstand dirt, grease, grime, linguini on the kitchen wall, socks on the floor and cigars everywhere.

Then, the neatnik won't leave a dirty dish in the sink overnight. Most of us are somewhere in between.

For me, it's the top of the piano. If I can see dust on top of the dark piano wood, then I get busy and do something. But until then, I'm pretty satisfied with the way things are. And what is *your* "dirt tolerance level"?

You may have another interesting person on the inside of you who is responsible for **Quality Control**. This character takes pride in doing something well. They continually ask, "Is it good enough?" Unfortunately, this character is also responsible for a lot of stalling maneuvers. You may not want to start an endeavor until you feel that you can do it perfectly. The internal Quality Control Director doesn't like risk and may prevent you from trying anything new.

These are the nine different Internal Directors or voices common to most of us. How these directors speak to us determines how we feel about ourselves and what our behavior will be. Whether we act or whether we sit depends on which voice is winning RIGHT NOW.

Also understand that you have more than just these nine voices. A conservative estimate would be more like 200 voices. All with different agendas. Now, understand that your spouse or your boss also has 200 voices. And maybe you agree on everything *but* there is just one area you can't seem to agree on. It is not surprising. Trying to match 400 directors at once can be plenty taxing. And you wonder why people aren't getting along.

"Listen to the still small voice within." That's nice advice but I don't get a "still small voice," I get a chorus! So do you.

It will help if you think of yourself as a company president and that you preside over a group of vice-presidents or directors. Each one of these directors is responsible for a different area of your life. And just like any normal company, these directors are going to be at cross purposes sometimes. Your job is to mediate and negotiate and direct peaceful settlements between your Internal Directors and keep the company AS A WHOLE healthy.

Who *are* these directors?

They are your Survival Mechanisms. And that's what they are doing inside of your head. They all have different ideas about what constitutes your survival, however. And they can be difficult to listen to because they use words like: "should," "must," "have to," and "ought to." They are frequently demanding and unreasonable. Survival Mechanisms are rarely logical. They have their own ideas. And they are all vying for attention and air time in your head.

Take this little scene...

You have read your latest issue of *Prevention Magazine* and you have your list of vitamins, minerals and supplements that you're supposed to take. You are now standing in the vitamin section of the health food store and you are beginning to fill your cart. Okay, there's $6.89 for some calcium...and here's a bottle of Vitamin C for $5.50...and the selenium is $4.69...and hmmmmm, the Vitamin E is another $6.00

Pretty soon you look for and purchase a multi-vitamin for around $10.00, saying to yourself, "Oh, this is probably good enough."

What happened?

Well, your Health Director and your Finance Director fought it out and there was a compromise. "Yes, I want to be healthy and vitaminized...but I don't want to go to the Poorhouse to do it." And the compromise happened so quickly that you weren't even aware of it.

See how it works?

These directors are constantly at work directing *your* life.

Everyday life is a series of these compromises. Sometimes you like the compromise, but often something inside of you is left wanting. If this internal "wanting" goes on long enough and it is important enough, sabotage is the result.

SELF-SABOTAGE IS WHEN TWO OR MORE INTERNAL DIRECTORS ARE FIGHTING EACH OTHER.

And you are the last one to know.

What can be gained by communicating with your Internal Directors?

Remember the advice, "Know thyself"? Well, we didn't come with an Instruction Manual.

We appear to be complex, inconsistent, often irrational, self-defeating and confused. We do not understand why we lose weight and gain it back. We start projects and never finish. We intend to do "good works" and never seem to get to it. In short, we are a mystery to ourselves.

What can be gained by a *dialogue* with your Internal Directors is understanding about *what motivates you*. Instead of making no sense, you will begin to see that you make a lot of sense. Your directors, if allowed to speak to you, will tell you why you do what you do.

Whatever your reasons are, a conversation with your internal directors will provide you with information that allows you to "know thyself."

Want to meet your internal directors now?

I am going to ask you a question and after you read the question, look up from this book and listen for 7 seconds. Take what you get. Ready?

If your Financial Director were sitting in front of you right now, what is the one thing this person would have to say to you?

? ? ? ? ? ? ? ? ? ? ? ? ? ? ? ? ? ? ? ?

Now, did you get a pat on the back?

Or did you get yelled at?

Or did you get a little pep talk...a kind of "you could do better if you tried" sort of speech?

Was there anger?

Did you get a gold star?

Now, let's pick another one... Again, read the question and then look up from this book and think about the question for about 7 seconds and listen for the internal response. Ready?

Your Health Director is now seated in front of you. What is the one thing that your Health Director would have to say to you?

? ? ? ? ? ? ? ? ? ? ? ? ? ? ? ? ? ? ? ?

Now let's go to your old friend the P.R. Director.

What is the one thing that your P.R. Director would have to say to you?

? ? ? ? ? ? ? ? ? ? ? ? ? ? ? ? ? ? ?

How did you do with the Health Director?

Did you get a pat on the back? No? What are the expectations of this director? Did you get the message that you're supposed to exercise? Or go in for a physical? Or lose a little weight?

Was there anger?

Did the Time Keeper jump into the conversation?

("No, I don't have time to exercise....")

Did the Financial Director get into it?

("I don't want to spend the money on dental bills right now....")

Did you get a gold star from the Health Director?

And how are your Public Relations? What did the P.R. Director have to say to you?

Get a pat on the back..."you're OK, kid?"

Or something like..."I wish you'd get rid of that ratty raincoat."

If you are trying to read this book while riding in a plane or on a bus or a train...have you tried to hide the title from the other passengers? God forbid you should admit to procrastinating. Or that anybody should see that you think maybe that you might!

THREE WAYS OF COMMUNICATING WITH INTERNAL DIRECTORS:

Way #1

Set aside a few minutes of quiet time, uninterrupted time. Your brain works *very fast* so not much time is required.

Close your eyes. (Optional.)

Imagine the inside of a theatre. Picture in your mind: the color of the walls, the fabric of the theatre seats, the size of the stage, the type of floor covering, and any details. See the stage and the chair that is in the center of the stage. Make it a comfortable chair. Sit in the chair. Look out across the theatre. Imagine that your internal directors occupy the theatre seats.

Ask to speak to the director in charge of whatever issue you would like to discuss.

When this director acknowledges, thank them. Ask them if they would be willing to communicate with you about the issue. When they say "yes," thank them.

You are now *in a negotiation*. It is not unlike union and management negotiations. Or price dickering over a car. Or the negotiating that goes on at the United Nations.

It would help if you could be: respectful, courteous, thoughtful, understanding and firm.

Negotiate a settlement with this internal director. Frequently other internal directors will join in the conversation and you will have to mediate. If the issue you are working on is a sabotage issue, then clearly it is because "part of you wants one thing and part of you wants something else."

HAVE A DIALOGUE IN YOUR MIND.

Way #2

Go to see a trusted friend, counselor or therapist. Explain to them what I have explained to you in this chapter...about your internal directors. Or give this person a copy of Chapter 2. Have this person lead you through a negotiation with your internal directors. Have them help you "make a deal" regarding your future behavior with your internal directors.

HAVE A DIALOGUE WITH SOMEONE ELSE.

Way #3

Sit down at a desk or table with:

1. a typewriter,
2. a computer,
3. a pen and pad,
4. or a blank book.

You are about to write a script.

If you want to speak to the Financial Director, for example, write "F.D.:" and then record everything that you hear from the Financial Director. Write your name or initial and speak back to this director. Listen and record. Speak your mind on paper. Compromise, settle disagreements, NEGOTIATE.

HAVE A DIALOGUE ON PAPER.

(Sometimes what you write may be something that you would like to *keep secret*. When confidentiality is an issue, take steps to insure your privacy. The most trustworthy husband or wife will have difficulty keeping their hands and eyes out of your journal. Solve this problem before you begin...otherwise it will affect the quality of the intimacy that you are trying to establish in your Inner Theatre. Using computers for this inner work is especially advantageous because of the size of a floppy disk and the programmable lockouts of some systems.)

When you establish contact with your own inner directors you will be meeting some of the most fascinating characters that you will *ever* meet. Other forms of entertainment will pale by comparison. The plastic people that you see on television every night will not interest you half as much as the unusual group of characters that reside in your Inner Theatre. And unlike television, this activity is *interactive*... you get to talk with these characters.

You'll never be alone again either.

And you can take your Inner Theatre and your Cast of Characters everywhere with you. Say, for instance, when you buy a car. Maybe the last time you bought a car, it was your P.R. Director's choice of a car. And this time you'd prefer that the Financial Director come along. Or maybe you're house-hunting and you would like to make a clear-headed decision about such an important purchase. You would appreciate it if your Internal Mom would be less vocal when you tour houses.

When you honor and respect the voices in your head, you will establish rapport and eventually become confidants and then, of course, be able to persuade. You'll be in a much better position to *influence yourself*.

(Isn't it remarkable the amount of information and the number of seminars and courses available about influencing other people? And yet, wouldn't it be great if we could just *influence ourselves*?)

THE WEIGHT SABOTAGE: Special Section

Nearly 45% of Americans are overweight and another 45% *think* they're overweight. If you are one of the 10% who does *not* have a concern about weight and/or body size, then go on to the next chapter.

For the 90% who are puzzled, frustrated and even angry about their weight (or a spouse's weight problem), you will find this special section interesting for three reasons:
1. The nature and complexity of this particular self-sabotage.
2. The lack of success in overcoming this sabotage.
3. The application of the Inner Theatre technique in understanding the challenge.

I chose to discuss the Weight Sabotage specifically because of three reasons of my own:
1. It is easy to identify. We are wearing the evidence around our middles.
2. It appears to be a difficult or at least, a challenging problem.
3. I have maintained a nearly 100 pound weight loss for over 10 years.

Let's take each of these in turn.

Easy to Identify

Self-sabotage is not always obvious. We may have sabotaged a job or a relationship and never knew that we were sabotaging.

But with weight, we know. Either we weigh what we want to weigh or we don't. And, unless we are being force-fed, this is clearly self-sabotage because we are *doing it to ourselves*. Even prisoners, who are deprived of most activities, can go on hunger strikes. It can only be considered self-sabotage when we have clear options and we take the undesirable one...repeatedly. When we say,

"I want to lose ten pounds," and then reach for a donut instead of an apple, we are selecting the sabotage.

"My mother overfed me as a baby," doesn't work if mom is no longer cooking for you and you are no longer a baby.

Appears to be Difficult

Your chances of overcoming obesity are less than your chances of overcoming cancer. Depending on which study you read, only 3% to 5% of the 17 million people who try are able to lose even 20 pounds and keep it off for a year.

Depressing? Maybe. But I have logged over 300 hours listening to compulsive overeaters describe their lives and I have met many people who have taken off over 80 pounds and have kept it off. I have seen "ordinary" people do what appears to be "extra-ordinary" things.

Another thought: If there are 5% who are successful, then why not decide that you can be one of those 5%?

My 100 Pounds

So statistically speaking, I'm one in a million.

I was a normal-weight baby but by age 7, I weighed over 100 pounds. I probably weigh less now than I did in the fifth grade. I was a hefty teenager and up until 1971, I was always interested in fad diets and any ad that promised a way to lose the weight. In January 1971 after a small weight loss, I weighed in at my doctor's office at well over 200 pounds.

1986 photograph of Alyce P. Cornyn-Selby before and after the peaceful negotiation with her Inner Theatre. Photo at left was taken in 1971.

The Nature of the Problem

Don't believe anyone who tries to tell you why you have your weight on. You are the only one who knows. And the reasons probably baffle you.

For every person who has the weight on, there is another reason to have it on. This is an extremely complex issue. So whatever the cause of your sabotage, it will be uniquely yours. Perhaps that is why it is so difficult to "treat."

I have a different perspective about fat. I think that it is doing something *for* us. The task is to find out *what*.

This idea may be so new and so radical to you that you resist it as you read it. The idea that I should suggest that your extra weight has a benefit to you is, well, ridiculous. You may even begin to feel anger at the idea that what you have been trying to get rid of all these years is actually something that you'd need.

Exercise assignment. Take a few moments and write a letter to your fat. Just write, Dear Fat, and see what comes to mind and write, write, write.

There are fascinating reasons why people have their fat. And instead of hate mail, the "Dear Fat" letters are filled with gratitude and understanding. This is a real peace-of-mind exercise and can be the beginning of getting the fat to move, if you chose it.

Just for a moment, pretend that you have your

weight on *for a very good reason.* Just pretend. If that reason were known to your friends, co-workers and relatives, they would all applaud you and say, "that's an excellent reason." No one would try to take your fat away and no one would suggest that you lose it if they knew this "very good reason."

I never suggest that anyone lose their weight. It is okay with me if anyone has extra pounds on...100, even 200 extra pounds. Because I believe that the weight is there for a very good reason...a reason that I don't know and probably a reason that they don't know.

If someone wants to lose weight and they aren't (and there is nothing medically wrong), isn't it obvious that SOMEONE ON THE INSIDE WANTS THE WEIGHT ON? The person on the inside *believes* that having the weight on *is a good idea*.

I believe that you have some rights. You have a right to weigh whatever it is that you weigh now. Get that number in mind. Repeat out loud: "I have a right to weigh _____ pounds."

I also believe in your right to change. You have a right to weigh whatever you *want* to weigh. Get that number in mind. Repeat out loud: "I have a right to weigh _____ pounds."

Using the Inner Theatre to Affect a Weight Change:

Imagine...you are sitting in the chair that is in the middle of your stage. It is a comfortable chair and you are looking out on your audience of internal directors. Perhaps this is the first time you have come to communicate in the Inner Theatre...or maybe you're an old hand at it.

Ask to speak to the person who is responsible for your weight. When this person acknowledges you, thank them for speaking up.

Then ask: Would you be willing to communicate with me about this?

When they say "yes," thank them.

Begin by acknowledging their function in your life (remember, they are one of your survival mechanisms.) You could say something like, "Thank you for taking care of me all of these years."

Explain that you would like to take off some weight and ask if they would help.

At this point, another inner director may stand up.

DO NOT ATTEMPT TO USE LOGIC IN YOUR INNER THEATRE.

Your directors may have some unreasonable, irrational and even amusing ideas about your survival and how they feel that they help you to survive. Don't try to change their minds. Accept whatever they tell you and work with that. They are entitled to their opinions and you can't strangle them or bully them or threaten. You *can* negotiate.

What if your inner directors are stubborn and irrational?

Have you ever negotiated with a stubborn and irrational person?

You see, if this were easy, a donkey could do it. If it all made sense, you would have had the weight off a long time ago. But you're still fat and your Fat Director is still winning.

You know that it is unhealthy and uncomfortable to have the weight on...and you still have it on. Where has your logical mind gotten you? Your logical mind wasn't around to help you stop smoking either.

Instead, your Fat Director is doing an excellent job and now you must deal with her/him. Other directors may object to your losing the weight also. It may put additional pressure on them. Your Sexual Director may be threatened. Your internal director responsible for your monogomy may be terrified. Your director in charge of Family Relationships may see problems ahead for you if you lose the weight. (Example: if everyone in your family is fat and you lose your weight, that is the same as telling them that they are *wrong*. If you've never told your family that they are wrong before, this could be threatening.)

You may have an internal director who is in charge of Historical Traumas. This person keeps track of the awful moments in your life and remembers "what you weighed when." The Historical Trauma Director will try to keep you away from a certain number on the scales because they are afraid something that happened in the past will happen again.

By the time you're finished with your negotiations, you may be dealing with several directors.

AN AGREEMENT MUST BE MADE IN THE INNER THEATRE BEFORE A CHANGE IN BEHAVIOR WILL HAPPEN.

Once you have asked for support and received agreement, turn the problem over to the winner of the group. That will be the person who has been responsible for keeping the weight on. They are the winner, right? Or you'd have the weight OFF. Any good manager knows to give the most difficult task to the most effective person. So give the task of taking the weight off to the person who has kept it on.

If your negotiation and assignment is successful, you will begin seeing subtle changes in your behavior. You will no longer have to "white knuckle it" when it comes to food. You *know* what you're supposed to eat.

Time is important to your Inner Theatre. When you make an agreement, set a time limit on it. Agree to re-evaluate the situation in three months, for instance. If the weight has come off and you are having problems dealing with members of the opposite sex, you may want to re-evaluate your decision to lose the weight. The weight loss may have scared you a little because now you have proof that you can talk yourself into action. Any number of things can happen, so agree to check in and re-think your new situation.

As an added incentive, in my own personal negotiation, I agreed to GAIN THE WEIGHT BACK, if I didn't like the results I was getting. "Results" means "the way the world is treating you."

What Others Learned in Their Inner Theatres

Denny: "I had never before had a weight problem. I was a professional sports car driver for 15 years and I was having a good season. All of a sudeen I gained weight and I was almost too fat for my fire suit. My fat was telling me to get out of driving and go back to managing the pit crew."

Paul: "I feel a great deal of accomplishment when I run marathon races and I do well, very well, for someone who is over 40 and in a non-physical profession. The hours of training and running would take me away from my family and I felt guilty about this. Well, I get a back pain whenever I weigh 20 pounds more than I should, and I won't run when my back hurts. My extra weight was just the excuse I needed to stay home with the family."

Susan: "My fat ruined a career for me in sales. I turned to designing and building furniture. I started my own business. I kept the weight on to make sure that I'd never leave my business...I didn't want to give myself the option of going back."

Kim: "I beat the big one — cancer. Although I was out of danger, I had 25 extra pounds on and I was disgusted with myself when I couldn't get it off. I did this Inner Theatre technique and I remembered that all the people who were in chemotherapy with me were thin... and they all died. I was keeping the weight on *just in case* the cancer came back and I would need it some day."

Cheryl: "I'm a management consultant and I don't want to communicate 'cute'; I want to communicate 'substance.' These extra 15 pounds are helping to anchor me so that I can't be thrown off base. I'm going to stop fighting with myself about the weight."

Boker: "My girl friend Sue didn't like fat men. So on each business trip, I stayed away a little longer and came back a little fatter. Sue finally left me. I didn't know it at the time, but that's what I wanted all along."

Barb: "Twenty years ago I tried out for head cheerleader and I didn't get it. I put the weight on then and I've kept it on all these years as a form of rebellion. I have been rebelling against the Ideal Female look. I wanted (and still want) to be liked for *who* I am, not what I look like."

Patricia: "I was plump at my wedding and then gained 60 pounds. I was also very young when I married and I hadn't really had an opportunity to sow any wild oats. I discovered that the extra pounds were my way of keeping my distance from men. I didn't feel like I could trust myself and I wanted my marriage to work. Having the weight on was my 'very good reason.'"

Jeremy: "If you had a stick in front of you and a collie puppy in front of you, which one would you reach for first? Sure, the collie puppy. My survival mechanisms told me that if I wanted to get touched, I should look like a collie puppy. I have been built like a collie puppy most of my life because I wanted to be touched and I'm ready to try something different."

"All the answers you seek are within."
 — Zen quote

Until they "went within," none of these people had the foggiest idea why they carried their weight...from 15 pounds to 150 pounds. The Inner Theatre technique provides a framework for getting to know yourself. You have a "very good reason" for having the weight on... what is it?

The Finale

Once you know the "very good reason" for your weight, you can understand the message or the benefit of the weight. The next step sounds obvious: GIVE YOURSELF WHAT THE WEIGHT IS GIVING YOU.
Is there any way that you can get what you want *without* having the weight on?
Remember when I told you to get what you want? When you get what you want, then you won't be sabotaging to get it.
For some people, the weight keeps them out of situations that spell discomfort. For Denny, it meant a career change. For Patricia, it meant getting serious about assertiveness training. For Boker, it meant staying out of relationships that he didn't really want. For Cheryl it meant redefining "substance" in her work.

How to Support Someone Who is Losing Weight

If you want to support your spouse, lover, kids or relatives with their weight loss, ask them, "How can I support you in this?" And then listen. Do what they say.
Maybe what they'd really like is for you to shut up about it. Or maybe they'd appreciate it if you didn't bring cookies into the house for awhile. Or maybe they'd be tickled just to have you around to listen.

If you want to support co-workers with their weight loss, the best thing you can do is keep quiet about the weight and instead, notice something positive about their work.

It is embarrassing to be acknowledged in the work environment for "body size," even if the comment was well intended. "Gee, you're looking good" is not something everyone likes to hear while working. For some, it is enough to gain the weight back. Instead, an honest compliment about quality of work will go a long way to helping self-confidence and also, a feeling that things are *better*.

What is this weight stuff doing in a book about procrastination?

We have been at a loss trying to understand the Weight Sabotage in the past. We have also been at a loss when it comes to explaining our procrastination.

The Weight Sabotage and procrastination have three things in common:

1. They are both forms of self-sabotage.
2. They are both understandable in the Inner Theatre.
3. They both occur for a "very good reason."

Of what possible benefit could procrastination be?

Read on. And meet eight excellent "reasons" in the form of eight different procrastinating characters...

CHAPTER 3
PROCRASTINATION AS A CREATIVE ACT

Procrastination.
I love to do it.
I must.
I do it all the time.
I can *sleep* and still do it.
"I'm so good at it; I can even do it in my sleep."

Mostly I can do it when I'm in love.
'Cause I love...to do it.
To say I will...and then won't.
It's a lot like loving.

"I should do my life while I'm thinking of it."

'Cause given the option...I'll leave.
And wander off to do my Life.
I'll do it slow...or I'll do it fast.
But I will do my Life exactly unaccording to my plan.

Procrastination is one of the most effective and creative tools available to us to get what we want out of life.

Procrastination is efficient and can be learned by just about anybody.

Procrastination can achieve results not possible any other way.

In a culture that worships success and overachieving, it is difficult to believe that the mysterious force called "procrastination" can be anything good. And yet, in a culture that values *results*, procrastination becomes an understandable champion. How could putting things off get results?

What better way to get reassurance and sympathy from your co-workers than to wait til the last minute to finish that report? What better way to keep people at a distance than to procrastinate about maintaining relationships? How could you add more action to your life any better than running the deadline out on your work? What better way is there to hide your potential than to continue slamdunking projects at the last minute? And what more acceptable way is there to rebel — against your marriage or your employer — than putting off your chores?

Procrastination protects you in times of discomfort. It helps you tolerate an impossible environment. It's a convenient and easy-to-learn skill. Procrastination can help you win battles or create drama or say "no" to pushy people. As a communication device, procrastination is the champion for creativity and efficiency.

Procrastination has just suffered a lot of bad press, that's all. Few human activities can compare with the genius of procrastination.

Assertiveness Training aside, it is pretty difficult to communicate with most people much of the time. Procrastination, with its simple, easy-to-learn techniques, can communicate a variety of messages and still be called "procrastination."

This chapter will describe eight characters who deal with life on this planet, as we know it, by using the creative techniques available to us by simply putting things off. You will recognize yourself in several of the characters.

Guilt is the constant companion of the procrastinator...who hasn't read this book. Procrastination should be like fancy wheel covers for your car — an option. If this is so, then guilt too can be an option. While procrastination (once it is fully understood and appreciated) is a viable tool, guilt, on the other hand, is still a worn out old religious idea that hasn't found its niche in modern day American mental health. Guilt is a feeling and is, therefore, the CHOICE of the person feeling it. Procrastination, however, is an *action* (or lack of action) and the feelings about it are up to the individual.

I never recommend that people STOP PROCRASTINATING. If they did, they would lose an effective way of dealing with life.

There once was a successful man who received regional attention from scores of professional people simply by procrastinating. His repeated acts of putting things off resulted in offers from his fiancee to save his neck and offers from his parents to save his financial bacon. He could never seem to get things done on time whether it was a proposal or just the daily work at hand. He couldn't seem to keep his financial act together and procrastinated about car care until his late model car was pronounced terminal. He went bankrupt, of course, and got plenty of attention from people who ordinarily wouldn't call him — lawyers, tax collectors, bankers and accountants. His lady friend invited him to live with her when he lost it "all." And his parents were there to rescue and comfort him.

There is plenty of drama available in the world today if you are just willing to put things off the way that this man did.

He continues to run on a time clock that is about 23 hours off kilter. He is responsible for the increase in the blood pressure of several employers, clients and suppliers. His ex-partners and ex-spouses (there have been several) gather every now and then to toast their good fortune at having outlived their financial disasters with him and to nurse their healing ulcers. The I.R.S. comes around to make house calls and his kids have learned to take reliable public transportation.

This man is a creative genius. Not just in his field — he is an exceptional talent — but in his mastery of how he lives his life. He orchestrates his relationships with proper amounts of procrastination to keep some people at a comfortable distance while maintaining dependent rescue missions with others. He is an excellent example of how you too, if properly motivated, can improve the quality of stress in your life and, in fact, the lives of everyone around you.

How we use procrastination to get what we want has only recently been examined by behaviorists. And they are coming to some remarkable conclusions:

"Procrastinating on decisions and commitments can help you feel you are less vulnerable to someone else's power."

"If you really discover...your irrational beliefs about procrastinating... you almost certainly will lose your feelings of intense shame about it."

"Procrastination is a very subjective thing."

"Procrastination doesn't always imply an addiction to short-range hedonism."

Finally. Some common sense about the age-old practice of putting things off. We need to think differently about procrastination in order to understand it.

People are never more creative than when they are sabotaging their own efforts...and often never more *productive* than when they are *procrastinating*.

How many creative things have been developed, do you suppose, when there was a different task at hand? How do you know that Edison didn't invent the electric light when he was supposed to be cleaning the top of his desk? And the Wright Brothers...they had a business to run, for heaven's sake! While they were out flapping their wings, who was back at the shop working on the financial statements? And even Leonardo da Vinci...did you know that he had client work to do when he sat sketching ideas for what would become plans for the helicopter?

LIFE is what happens to us while we're procrastinating. And Life, of course, is loaded with creative acts. You get very creative when you're procrastinating. It is amazing how many things you can get done while you're avoiding doing whatever it is that you said you were going to do.

"If you'd like to be more creative, just look at the same thing as everyone else and 'think something different,' " writes Roger von Oech, founder and president of Creative Think and author of *A Whack On The Side Of The Head*.

Roger is right. In times like these when an apple is a computer and an actor is a president, we need a different way of sizing things up. Roger also writes, "There are times when you need to be creative to accomplish your objectives." And accomplishing objectives is what creative procrastination is all about.

A carefully planned procrastination strategy can help you gain acceptance by your peers when you begin to look too successful. Putting things off can actually be an effective way of maintaining your comfort zone and keeping you safe. It allows for inspiration. And procrastination *can* be efficient because if you don't do it maybe someone else *will*. And if you work in a large corporation, and you procrastinate, there are two things that will likely happen:

1. No one will notice.
2. Someone will come up with information that will cause a directive that will make that task unnecessary anyway.

At no time in our history has creativity been more honored and procrastination been more disgraced. Nearly 100 years ago it was a cardinal sin. Thomas De Quincey wrote in 1859: "If once a man indulges himself in murder, very soon he comes to think little of robbing; and from robbing he comes next to drinking and sabbath-breaking, and from that to incivility and procrastination."

The recent folderol about productivity in this country, however, has caused us to do as Roger suggests, namely that we "look at the same things and think something different." The time is now right for deeper observations into our acts of sabotage and, in particular, procrastination.

For a disciplined person, there are two possible outcomes when you leave to take out the garbage:

1. You don't get there.
2. You do get there.

For a procrastinator, there are also two possible outcomes for you and the garbage:

1. You don't get there and you agonize over it.
2. You do get there after much agonizing.

The purpose of this chapter is *not* to make disciplined people out of procrastinators. The purpose of this chapter is to take a closer look at what we have been calling procrastination, look for the creative benefit and *then*, if you still feel like agonizing, recommend a different book. Something like *Creative Guilt*.

"Show me what you *do*," said the wise sage, "and I will show you your life."

Show me what you avoid and I will show you your internal genius.

HOW TO USE THIS KIT

This kit is designed for people who don't have time to read a book.

Read the description of the character and if that isn't you, go on to the next character. If you're in doubt, check the Self-Talk Identification.

Each of the eight characteristic styles includes:

>Title and description
>
>Pay Value
>
>Prescription
>
>Identifying Self-Talk
>
>Wall Mottos
>
>Combat Tactics

"Wall Mottos" are sentences used to replace your current Self-Talk. Wall Mottos can be used as daily affirmations and have significant effects on changing behavior when placed where they will be seen often. Suggested spots are: car dashboard, typewriter/computer, bathroom mirror, refrigerator door, desk top, calendar/appointment book. Wall Mottos work on communicating with the subconscience mind and will have an effect whether you make a point of reading them daily or not...if they are in your environment, they are working. (By the way, do you have any negative programming slogans in your environment now? Like, "The hurrier I go, the behinder I get" or "I work well under pressure." Eliminate these, please, and replace them with thoughts about your life that you would prefer.)

Before beginning the Eight Procrastinating Styles, remember this one important thing:

Procrastination is more important to us than sex. It must be, we do it more often.

So here are creative procrastinators at work.

THE BACK BURNER PROCRASTINATOR

THE ACTION JUNKIE PROCRASTINATOR

THE REBELLIOUS PROCRASTINATOR

THE PERFECTIONIST PROCRASTINATOR

THE CRAZYMAKING PROCRASTINATOR

THE "NICE" PROCRASTINATOR

THE "DON'T RELY ON ME" PROCRASTINATOR

THE FEELING GOOD PROCRASTINATOR

LITTLE BO PEEP OR THE BACK BURNER PROCRASTINATOR

Little Bo Peep, lost her sheep
And can't tell where to find them.
Leave them alone and they'll come home,
Wagging their tails behind them."

The problem with the "leave them alone" or "leave it alone" technique to problem-solving is that it often works.

Any bureaucrat will tell you that if you put it off long enough, it no longer has to get done. And most scientists and artists will tell you that if you "sleep on it" that it may solve itself. All true.

Coming up with THE creative answer isn't always an instant sort of operation. Because creativity is illusive and unpredictable, waiting for it to "hit" seems like a good plan. Nearly everyone has a story of how they pondered a situation and after a good night's sleep, the perfect answer revealed itself the next morning in the shower.

And if you solve a problem too quickly — if you offer a solution immediately — quite often your solution will be held in suspect. It came too easy. For anything to be very good and worthwhile, it needs to be considered carefully and that usually means that it should take time.

In the study of persuasion, sales people are instructed *not* to come up with solutions too quickly.

Even when the sales person has what they know is the perfect answer, it will not increase their credibility if they offer it. Instead, they are encouraged to ask questions, get definitive answers and then, after pondering, offer solutions. When the buyer is a "thinker" and takes their time with their own considerations, the sales person is trained to match that pace. The longer the buyer takes to answer questions, the longer the sales person should take in responding with solutions.

So we are trained, slowly but surely, to misjudge our original impulses and we place a high priority on behavior that *looks like* we're thinking. One designer explained her experience with this phenomenon:

"I met with the client and I immediately saw the completed solution. I saw it typeset and designed and embossed. I saw the texture of the paper and I saw it being used successfully. I had synthesized everything my client had said from past meetings and wham! It came together. So I blurted out the solution with great enthusiasm.

"But my client was a methodical sort of person and I had forgotten that in my burst of creativity. The idea was a risk, but it was a brilliant solution. He wouldn't buy such an *instant* solution.

"So I went back to the drawing board and created six other ideas. One of them was great but it wasn't brilliant. He bought that. It felt 'well-thought-out' to him. So we produced it. I will always be sorry that he didn't go for the first idea that I had.

"I learned something from this. I learned that immediate behavior is *not* rewarded and that postponing things are. I'm a person of action so I don't like this, but I have to live with it. My clients think that creativity takes time. So I have to take the time...whether I need to or not."

This woman designer is well organized, very experienced and a successful, creative person. She doesn't want to be trained into procrastinating behavior and realizes that her environment encourages it.

Perhaps some early school experiences taught us the same things: better put it off to make it really good. Some of us have been told that the first idea (that comes so fast!) is not ever going to be the *right* idea. And we want to be right. It can't possibly be right if:

1. It came easy.
2. It came fast.

So let's put it on the Back Burner. Quite often, what would develop on the Back Burner is green and hairy and you wouldn't want to eat it. The Back Burner may be overloaded *now*. You can put it back there if you want to...just be aware that you may lose your passion for it in the waiting. Yes, a lot of good ideas develop on the Back Burner. And a lot simply evaporate in the cooking.

"I only write when I'm terribly inspired. I make sure that I'm terribly inspired every morning at nine o'clock."

This writer's approach goes against the notion that if we wait, a more right solution will present itself. This person simply says, "I'll do it and risk it."

The Bo Peep/Back Burner Procrastinators would rather do nothing than take the risk of making the wrong choice. In this way, putting it off works; it is the benefit. Never having to commit to an idea or an opinion is a safe strategy and procrastination will help. This act is extremely beneficial to the person who wants to remain free to choose any option. Remaining uncommitted means that you can move in any direction and not lose face. If you're always "still examining and still considering" then you don't have to confront and you are less vulnerable to criticism. Indeed, it means never having to say you're sorry...it got put on the Back Burner and nothing really developed. So the worst you can be accused of is that the Muse simply didn't hit you.

Deep inside the recesses of your mind may just possibly lurk the voice of "reason" that suggests that *not* doing the thing will actually solve it.

Planning a holiday party would be a good example of this. Wait long enough to get started on it and BINGO! The holiday has come and gone and you are off the hook for a lot of work that you didn't really want to do anyway.

"I postponed the raft trip all summer until finally, it was just too cold to go. My wife Helen is easily diverted and although she really wanted us to go...it's just another thing that will have to wait another year. I want to go...I think, but it's easier postponing a decision than it is getting myself set to go on a raft trip. What would I do if the rapids were too much...or there were snakes? It's easier saying that I'll get to the decision than it is to deal with all that other stuff."

Procrastination keeps Charlie away from the river and keeps the easily-diverted Helen still thinking well of Charlie. So he puts it off and stays dry. Helen is left with the impression that Charlie wants to go and that they will "get around to it" one of these summers.

"Tomorrow is another day," said Scarlett O'Hara. And for the most part, this approach worked for her. And it's probably been working for you...at least part of the time.

The mystique of waiting for the creative muse to strike is an idea that encourages us to procrastinate.

The idea that good decisions take time is another aid to justifying this type of procrastination. Tomorrow will bring more information and *then* we can make a good decision ... that's the third rationalization that keeps us Bo Peeping our way through life.

"I kept putting off the decision to move my office downtown," said the crackerjack attorney in a group seminar. "I thought that eventually some factor would show itself and then I'd be able to make a clear and intelligent decision. Months went by. I ran out of business cards waiting for something inside of me to finally decide. Nothing seemed to work."

Brian's story is typical. Something will come along and decide for us. That helps spread the responsibility to something other than ourselves.

Brian continued: "I remember waiting for the new mass transit system to be constructed. I wanted to see how that would work and if it would be successful. I had myself believing that I could analyze and think my way into a perfect solution. I finally got so embarrassed at not having business cards to hand out — I couldn't have the cards printed until I knew where my office would be — I finally sat down and decided to decide. I devoted five solid minutes to the problem and I had an answer. What amazed me was this: it took so little *time* when I finally got down to it!"

It is claimed that we human beings use only 10% of our brain power. I have no idea how this statistic was discovered or by what measurement it was taken...I believe in the awesome power of the human mind to THINK. I also believe that it takes time. Split seconds in most cases, but it takes time. Brian had been postponing what he thought would be a lengthy analysis. In five, *uninterrupted* minutes, however, he managed to ask himself everything he needed to know to make a decision.

Five minutes devoted totally to that decision could end your procrastination problems. With the incredible speed that our brains are capable of... five minutes may seem long for 90% of the decisions we've been postponing.

Take a look at the list that you have prepared from Chapter One. Read through the list until you find an item there that may be a Bo Peep/Back Burner procrastinated decision. Now give it five minutes. Ask questions of yourself and get answers. Write something.

Do it now.

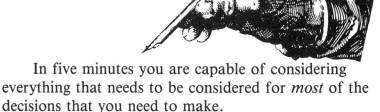

In five minutes you are capable of considering everything that needs to be considered for *most* of the decisions that you need to make.

And remember: RARELY DO WE HAVE *ALL* THE INFORMATION THAT WE NEED TO MAKE A DECISION.

If you are in a management position or if you are a parent, you know the experience of having to make a decision without all the information that you would like to have. You may never experience a situation where you have all the perfect and complete information with which you'd be comfortable making a decision. (This is supposed to be the Information Age, isn't it? Sometimes we feel guilty that we don't have the information to make the decision.)

A smart reason to procrastinate: "You don't have enough information to start or finish. Going ahead could mean wasted effort."

My next question would be:

When are you going to have the information?

If the answer is "probably never" then make the decision to decide...give yourself five minutes...and get on with it. Not having all the information is not a criminal situation. It's situation normal.

Ever notice how easy it is for you to comment on someone else's procrastination when it comes to decision-making? If you have a boss who procrastinates about decisions, you *know* that you wouldn't. There are two reasons for this:

1. You have more information than he/she does.
2. It doesn't matter to you that you don't have all the information.

"I really thought that making the decision about my vacation was an important one and I also thought that it would require a lot of my time to make this decision. Okay, okay. I decided to decide. I swear...I took out a sheet of paper and asked myself the questions that I needed to know and I had my decision in less than four minutes. I'll bet that I spent more brain power avoiding the decision because I thought that it was going to require so much of me. It didn't. I'm not afraid to just look at it and take the five minute decision test now. I really don't need to have all the information. I just need the time to decide. I was amazed at *how little* time that turned out to be."

This is 33-year-old Clair who makes major corporate decisions about large financial matters while she's waiting for elevators. Sometimes we're reluctant to move our decision-making ability from one area of our lives to another.

Tom, working at a temporary summer job, learned a valuable lesson that followed him back to the college campus where he worked as an instructor. Tom's course work centered around English composition and since most of his employment career had been spent in academia, he held strong to the myth of the muse. As a result, Tom dealt with his own "creative" procrastination and the procrastination of his students. Then one summer, Tom agreed to help a friend who owned a small advertising agency. Deadlines were not arbitrary and creativity was a marketable product. Tom quickly learned that his inspiration was not part of the fast-paced copywriting world and after awhile his creative juices began to flow on cue.

"I had been allowed to procrastinate...in fact, I think I may have been rewarded for it," said Tom. "I gained some self-confidence about my writing through having to move things from the Back Burner to the Hot Seat. I learned that I *can* come up with something on the spot and lingering over it *sometimes* gets a better solution, but certainly not always."

Tom now has a choice about his procrastination. He can wait for inspiration and take advantage of the added passion for his writing...or he can simply begin and see what happens.

Focus. Such a simple concept. And yet, Back Burner training tells us *not* to focus. The ability to focus, however, has been identified as one of the essential qualities of successful entrepreneurs. Their "magic" may come from a habit of short range "focusing." They have been compared to heat-seeking missiles.

The Five Minute Focus. You'll spend more time trying to avoid it. Now the jig is up and the rationalizations about it can be put aside. You don't need to wait for the muse to hit you. If you're Bo Peep you can go look for the sheep if you want to...and if you've got it on the Back Burner, it's either time to serve it up or throw it out.

THE PAY VALUE: for the Back Burner Procrastinator is false security and the mistaken idea that more time will mean the deliverance of a better idea.

THE PRESCRIPTION: for the Back Burner Procrastinator is uninterrupted focus and a deadline.

Identifying the Self-Talk of a Bo-Peep/Back Burner

"This decision is going to take a lot of time — I'd better wait."

"I need more information before I can do anything."

"Maybe something will come up that will change things."

"Leave it alone...it'll probably solve itself."

"Leave it alone...a creative solution will pop up."

"I'll get inspired later."

"I can't be creative on cue."

"Put it on the Back Burner and let it cook for awhile."

"I'd better not solve this problem too fast."

"I can't think on my feet."

"It had better be right — I'd better wait."

"If I wait long enough, I won't have to decide."

"If I decide, I won't get a chance to redecide... I'll be stuck with this forever."

WALL MOTTOS
FOR BACK BURNER PROCRASTINATORS

(Post in convenient place. For greater effect, recite daily *aloud*. Replace your current Self-Talk with...)

"Some questions cannot be answered,
but they can be decided."
— *Harry Truman*

"Not deciding *is* making a decision."
— *Travis Duncan*

"Nothing would be done at all if we waited for all the information."
— *Z. Bohachi*

"What the hell...might as well do it."
— *Susan Marcus*

AFFIRMATIONS

For today, it is enough just to do.

What is the worst that could happen?

The time is now.

I am willing to take responsibility for my actions.

I make good decisions and things turn out well for me.

COMBAT TACTICS
FOR BACK BURNER PROCRASTINATORS

If you have identified yourself as a possible Bo Peep procrastinator and you also have a few too many things on the Back Burner, do the following:

1. Ask yourself: Do I have enough information to make a decision or do this task?

2. Ask yourself: Will I ever have enough information to make this decision or do this task?

   (If the answer to this question is "Yes," then your next step is to gather the information needed. Now you are no longer in the decision-making mode and therefore, no longer procrastinating. What do you need to make the decision or to act? Are you going to get the information that you need? Now, be honest. If you're really not interested in gathering the information and you know that you'd rather make the decision without it, then go ahead.)

3. Execute the Five Minute Focus.

   Give yourself five minutes of uninterrupted TIME. Know that at the end of five minutes some sort of action will take place. Give your mind the opportunity to fondle the situation and not simply skirt the issues.

THE ACTION JUNKIE PROCRASTINATOR

If all the calendars and timepieces in the world were suddenly destroyed, most of us would be grateful for about fifteen minutes. After half an hour, some of us would be very nervous and by the end of two hours most of us would be stark raving nuts.

The simple fact is: we love deadlines.

Most of us can't get motivated without one. We simply aren't interested.

Carl Jung called this type of person a Sensor Personality. A whopping 40% of us are in this category — the largest of the four personality groupings devised by Jung. The Sensor's whole life revolves around time and what to do with it. Tracking time is important to this person...hence the great success of the organization calendar books that fast-trackers all carry now. "Here let me check my appointment book." "I've got to look at the Book first." "I'll write you in the Book." "Now shall I pencil in that lunch on Tuesday?"

Action. It's really one of the cornerstone characteristics of the American operating philosophy, isn't it? We fell in love with Errol Flynn, modeled John Wayne and dressed like Indiana Jones. As consumers, what we don't spend on food, we spend on some sort of action — buying a television set to watch it all on, exercise equipment to make it happen indoors or cars that look like they're going 50 m.p.h. while they're still parked. We work like crazy 50 weeks of the year and then take two weeks off and do what with it? Relax? Not on your tintype! If you're a typical American, you'll load up the car and the kid(s) and head out for a little action.

Nobody really wants to be the Maytag repairman.

Procrastination is a creative way of buying yourself a little action. It's easier to get excited when the due date is the day after tomorrow.

Which brings us to the phenomenon of proximity of space and time. Consider this...

"There's been a plane crash."

"Where?"

"About two miles off the coast of Botwa...about 11,000 miles from here."

"So?"

OR

"There's been a plane crash."

"Where?"

"Three doors down from your house."

In terms of proximity of space, we have no trouble getting excited about anything that happens *near* us. There is a corresponding phenomenon with time.

"I was in a car wreck."

"When?"

"About six years ago..."

OR

"I was in a car wreck."

"When?"

"Just now! It just happened!"

If the event is *near* us in either space or time, we give it greater importance in our lives. The importance of the event is graded primarily on its proximity of space and time.

Remember the cartoon of the character in the cannon with the caption: "I work well under pressure." The truth is, many of us cannot work at all unless there is pressure — and that means proximity of time — the nearness of the due date.

Creative procrastination provides *drama* in our lives. Most of us can't stand to have things running too smoothly for very long and procrastination provides excitement and pressure that we all need. Why do you procrastinate? Look at the possibility that you may be an Action Junkie.

I worked for a man once who blew up every morning at nine o'clock. He was an older fellow and the way that he had the world arranged in his head was: to be seen as important, you must have problems. All the role models he had ever had, the people in the organization that were earning the big salaries...they also had the big problems. His mentor could have been Mr. Dithers, Dagwood's boss. Problems, of course, weren't worth having unless you could frown and fret about them and make sure that everyone knew about the problems.

There's nothing wrong with this arrangement. It was a system of dealing with corporate life that seemed to pay off for him. When he retired, however, his position wasn't filled and somehow the problems went away too.

Some people get off on their own adrenalin. Adrenalin is a drug...it's like giving yourself a shot of power. It's stimulating. Continued use and abuse, however, like most drugs, begins to look like addiction.

So...we need that little fix and we need it on two levels. One is physiological: a self-generating drug. And the other is emotional: self-generating worth. Action Junkies aren't stupid. They know a good thing when they see it. Procrastination is a perfect tool for creating a bit of *action*.

A woman who is vice-president of a banking conglomerate talks about her mother: "No matter what I do or how successful I get, I will always have the perspective that my mother can run circles around me. She is always involved in a fight. She is battling for a cause, or with the I.R.S., or with a supplier. I don't know how she does it. I could not keep up that kind of pace. Every time I talk with her she has a new battle and a new deadline going."

Mom is addicted to her own adrenalin just like my old boss was. We're a whole lot more important when we have a deadline upon us — someone needs something from us RIGHT AWAY! — and it feels good to have a full head of steam going.

Stress. It is a much-written-about topic. Rarely can you make it through the grocery checkout line without reading a headline about stress and the new ill that it will cause. Much of that stress is self-induced and there's a good reason for it. "Stress without distress is motivation." Nothing will motivate you faster than a gun to your head and running the time frame out and looking down the barrel of a deadline motivates a lot of us.

Doug was given ten days to prepare for leading an important managers' meeting for his firm. "I frittered away the week," he explained, "minor procrastinating...and then I really loafed on the weekend...major procrastinating. I got up at 4 a.m. Monday morning to begin drawing up the charts for the meeting. And I felt absolutely alive. It came together beautifully.

"Thinking about it now...I am in a job that sees very little completion of tasks; they're really ongoing. It felt *great* to have something that would have a beginning, a middle and an end. I relished it.

"Ordinarily I wouldn't act this way. Running out the time that way...there's no margin for error...and if something else had come up...ANYTHING ELSE...like catching the flu or having to give my wife a ride to work because her car wouldn't start...just anything...I wouldn't have made it."

Doug resolved his own desire for action as he finished his story. Getting involved with faster moving projects became his personal career goal. Although he enjoyed his thrilling procrastination and his success at the managers' meeting, he recognized a deeper motivation.

Putting it off allows a procrastinator to put some importance to the task. With a crushing deadline, we're far more important and far more active. You probably learned this when you were in school — when you were bored. It was a way of livening things up a little.

Nolan Bushnell, founder of Atari, Inc., and recognized star in the creativity department, wrote the foreword for Roger von Oech's book on creativity, *A Whack On The Side Of The Head*. He epitomizes the Action Junkie when he says, "I like to set difficult deadlines for myself. That's because I believe that *the ultimate inspiration is the deadline.*"

THE PAY VALUE: for the Action Junkie Procrastinator is increased drama and action.

THE PRESCRIPTION: for the Action Junkie Procrastinator is adding more excitement to life. Give yourself what you're craving...action.

Identifying the Self-Talk of the Action Junkie

"I love a challenge."

"If I can do it this time, it'll be a miracle."

"I've got only _____ to do _____!"
                    (time)   (task)

"If I get started on Sunday, I can still make it."

"I can pull it off."

"I've never let anybody down."

"I work well under presssure."

"I wonder if I'm going to make it this time."

"I bet it won't take long to do that."

"It's amazing how little time I can spend on this and have everybody think it's super. (Fools.)"

"Give me a dozen things to do and I can get them all done. But give me one or two things to do and I can't seem to do anything."

WALL MOTTOS FOR ACTION JUNKIES

(Post in convenient place. For greater effect, recite daily *aloud*. Replace your current Self-Talk with...)

"I've had a lot of problems in my day — most of which never happened."
— *Mark Twain*

"Time flies when you're unconscious."
— *Matt Simek*

"There's a difference between activity and accomplishment."
— *Travis Duncan*

"It is not the flapping of the hen that lays the egg."
— *Egyptian proverb*

AFFIRMATIONS

There is enough (time, money, energy). What I am doing is enough.

Release, relax, enjoy. (Repeated in 3 exhales).

I can live my life efficiently today.

I do what is necessary when it is necessary.

All I can do is all I can do.

My life moves at a comfortable pace.

I complete work gracefully and on time.

COMBAT TACTICS FOR ACTION JUNKIES

If you have identified yourself as a possible Action Junkie procrastinator, do the following:

1. Ask yourself: What is the pressure doing for me? Translate this benefit into a different form of action: take up skydiving, driving a cab in New York, hostage negotiating or babysitting small children. If action is what you crave, use your creative thinking abilities to get you the same action without risking the tasks that are really important to you. Understand that your need for action *varies* too. If you are working on a particularly long project that lacks action, you may want to *increase* your action activities in another area of your life. Like the doctoral thesis student who took up white water river rafting until she had her Ph.D. in hand.

2. This type of procrastinating requires FORCED FOCUS. (See description of Bo Peep and the Back Burners...not a rock group.)

   Ask yourself: can I get focused any other way ...besides running the deadline?

   (Perhaps you need to change your environment, your schedule or even your love life. What else in your life causes you to get focused without the time frame being a factor?)

3. Ask yourself: Is this my pace or someone else's pace (Mom's, Dad's, your boss's, a teacher's)?

   You have the right to live your life at your own pace...however juiced up that may be at this moment. Are *you* really happy with it? Or do you feel that this pace is necessary in order to impress upon everyone how *very* important your work is?

An Action Junkie may also be hooked on accomplishments. It feels *so good* when the thing is complete! If completion is part of your action and your satisfaction, then consider "chunking down" a task. No matter how small a task is...it is possible to get it into even smaller chunks. Washing the cat, for instance, can be "chunked down" into tiny action bits. Go get the washtub. Go find the flea shampoo. Get drugs for the cat and the first aid kit for yourself. Then do nothing. The cat doesn't have to be washed until Tuesday.

There is no problem too small but what it can't be chunked down. Turn your inner Action Junkie into an Accomplishment Junkie.

THE REBELLIOUS PROCRASTINATOR:
I Don't Want To And You Can't Make Me...

"I procrastinate because I don't want to do it! It's as simple as that! I just don't *want* to clean out the garage! Nothing too complicated about *that*!"

Right. You probably wouldn't find me hurrying to sign up for that job myself. But it's *your* list. Procrastination is assigning yourself the task and then making sure that it doesn't get done. If "to clean the garage" is the item on this list...then you put it there.

There is a greater dynamic going on here, however. Especially for those procrastinators who were the young and impressionable youth of the 1960's. This was a time when acting like a mule received applause. Smoke cigars in the university president's captured office or drop a daisy down the barrel of an M-16 rifle. "Hell, no, we won't go!" was the response to *everything* from going to the bathroom to going to war. "I don't have to" was the wall motto of the decade and "You can't make me" was its bumper sticker cousin. The "IN" word was "anti-" and it was applied to perspirants and aircraft guns.

Even though most of that population now votes Republican, buys IRA's, goes bowling and may drive a Volvo, that inner 1960's voice is still with us. And it causes us to procrastinate. Procrastination is a way of saying, "You can't make me do this...at least not right now." By using procrastination to resist anything (self-imposed or external), you may be asserting what little control you may feel you still have in your life — that *you* are still your own person.

For the rebellious procrastinator, the battlefield is the work place, a marriage, parenthood and even friendship. Things like the phone bill, a parking ticket, library fines and April 15 are all symbols of authority and are clearly lines drawn. To simply comply is losing the opportunity to defy authority. "Fasten your seat belts" may light up on the dashboard of the Rebellious Procrastinator's car and the internal response is, "You can't make me."

Rebellious procrastination is not restricted to the Flower Children of Yesteryear, but is a distinctive American trait. We come from generations of survivors who question everything to a hung jury. You don't find placid people turning colonies into nations and you don't see them saddling up to come West either. It is part of the American character to rebel. We worship the hero who takes a stance against all odds...a few movies come immediately to mind: *Sometimes A Great Notion, Rambo, On the Waterfront, Norma Rae.* It's a pretty popular theme and many of us were literally trained by our parents to express rebellion. Unfortunately they didn't always show us how to do it gracefully.

Phil was a 26-year-old glass cutter, married with one child and a raving case of rebellious procrastination. Since no one had taught Phil just how to rebel, he had created his own solutions and procrastination figured heavily into it. Phil was rarely on time for anything since to be his own timekeeper proved internally that he was "his own man." Parking meters were little metal authority figures lined up on the street. Phil ignored them and the tickets *and* the letters from the city with the computerized results. He "forgot" to pay the water bill and his taxes. A soft-spoken and respectful person, Phil paid a high price for his rebellion as he lost two jobs and nearly ended his marriage.

Creative procrastination is often a way of saying: "I don't like this" (frustration, irritation) and "You can't tell me what to do" (independence, freedom-fighter). And all this can happen WITHOUT conscious awareness. Our procrastination is a complete mystery to us, although we might be the first to admit that we're a *little* rebellious. It doesn't have to be as extreme as Phil's procrastination. Take a look at your list developed from Chapter One. Is there a pattern emerging from the list? Do you joust with windmills — that is, procrastinate against some form of authority figure who doesn't even know you? Taxes. If you ask for an extension every year, or simply refuse to pay them at all, what are you really saying with your procrastination?

One architect I know does what he calls "getting by on float." That means that he refuses to pay his bills for as long as he can, getting by and sitting on the money that has been paid to him. He proudly claims that he can get by for a year "on float." This is another way of saying, "I worked for it. I have it. And I'm going to keep it as long as I can."

What is the message in your procrastination?

For the Rebellious Procrastinator, an internal voice states a goal and another unconscious voice says, "I don't have to and you can't make me." The "To Do" List for the day becomes the parent and we become the brat. Our own goals become something to beat...to overcome. That's why Goal Setting workshops rarely work for these special procrastinators. In our effort to express our freedom by procrastinating, we actually restrict our freedom. By not going along...at least some of the time...we alienate people, make employment difficult, drive spouses crazy and lose control of what we really want in life.

Procrastination is a way of expressing our displeasure with a world that doesn't make a great deal of sense much of the time and "forces" us to do things that we don't want to do. Putting it off is a superb strategy for a mule. And it works for people too.

"We're all such good little girls, such brave, stalwart little boys, such polite little children—" writes Barbara Sher in *Wishcraft: How to Get What You Really Want*, "and inside every one of us is an obnoxious little brat, just squirming to be let out. That brat is your baby, and you'd better love this person, because you ignore them at your peril."

I agree. I have what I call a "well-developed teenager" on the inside and I let that character have its voice. It's bigger than a baby and can be as stubborn as a terrorist. My inner teenager is the one who rebels against everything. If I get a notice from my dentist that I'm due for a checkup, I procrastinate just to let my dentist know that I'm really in charge. Now, my dentist never really gets that message but that doesn't really matter. When I'm in the chair, he's got me. But I'm still me until I get there.

Mary Ellen's car is always late for its mileage checkups. Mary Ellen doesn't know anything about cars and she knows that she doesn't know anything about cars and she resents the fact that the car mechanics know and she doesn't know what makes the car run. To express her vulnerability with the situation and her own displeasure at their knowing and her not knowing, she procrastinates about getting her car checked. Mary Ellen is a competent businesswoman with a successful career in a law firm... and a Volvo that's barely hanging in there.

Rebellion-by-procrastination shows up most vividly in employment situations. The military system of power is the most popularly used structure in most organizations and this is a perfect breeding ground for the procrastination acts of the rebellious. Trying to deal with the procrastinating employee can be taxing for the most patient manager. Authority can leave the rebellious procrastinator feeling helpless and unequal. To help balance this inequality, they put off doing work... even work they like to do. The message is, "I'll do it, but I'll do it in my own good time." Procrastination is a way of bringing the balance of power back to the employee. Frequently, a talented employee can be a deft enough procrastinator to avoid being fired, but come close very often. The excuses for procrastinating behavior would make a practicing alcoholic blush and a classic case of the "forget's" is a good stand-by. Sometimes an employee will feel that a task is unnecessary or an intrusion on their regular work. A natural reaction is to shove it aside.

Sharon is a procrastinator whose battlefield was the boardroom. "I didn't want to take minutes of the meeting. After three months of late meeting notices, they gave the job to somebody else." Sharon got what she wanted. But at what cost? Rebelling against co-workers, superiors, bosses, management-in-general and authority specifically is not the issue here. Choosing the way to rebel (nobody taught us how) is the challenge. Procrastination is one way to show authority how little we appreciate the intrusion. There are other ways.

THE PAY VALUE: for the Rebellious Procrastinator is a chance to express anger and rebellion...often justified and long overdue.

THE PRESCRIPTION: for the Rebellious Procrastinator is to find ways to rebel, to express displeasure and anger. What seems to help Rebellious Procrastinators the most is an increase in the feeling of control in their lives.

IDENTIFYING THE SELF-TALK
OF THE REBELLIOUS PROCRASTINATOR

"I don't have to."

"I don't want to."

"You can't make me."

"Maybe later."

"We'll see."

"I know I'm *supposed* to!"

"I shouldn't have to do this."

"Why does this happen to *me*?"

"Rules are made to be broken."

"I'm special."

"I don't really have to do this."

WALL MOTTOS
FOR REBELLIOUS PROCRASTINATORS

(Post in convenient place. For greater effect, recite daily *aloud*. Replace your current Self-Talk with...)

"If you feed a dog, it won't bite you. That is the principle difference between a dog and a man."
—*Mark Twain*

"They never erected a statue to those people who let well enough alone."
—*Unknown*

"Outlaw or statesman...'tis a fine line in a rebellious nature."
—*T. D. Duncan*

AFFIRMATIONS

My life works for me.

I can communicate an uncomfortable message well.

There is a way to let people know and I will find the graceful way.

I am having a positive effect.

I admire my spirit and use it for good.

I am free.

This is *my day*.

I have a right to my own time.

COMBAT TACTICS
FOR REBELLIOUS PROCRASTINATORS

If you have identified yourself as a possible Rebellious Procrastinator, do the following:
1. Take your rebelliousness out on something besides your "To Do" List. Learn to write letters to your congressmen, attend neighborhood association meetings, back a political candidate, write for an underground newspaper — do any productive rebellious thing that you can think of...just get it out of your system. Sing one more round of "We Shall Overcome" and then get back to work.

2. Understand the remarkable freedom that comes with assertiveness skills. Learn how to say, "No, I don't want to do that."

3. If you are a rebellious procrastinator at work: Understand that if you have agreed to work for a company, then you have agreed to play by their rules. And if you have agreed to play by their rules, then whose rules are they? They're *your* rules, that's whose.

   If you can't stand the rules,
   DON'T CASH YOUR PAYCHECK.

4. Don't set yourself up for failure...put only things that you really want to do on your "To Do" List. (It's okay for you not to like the task...all that is required is a desire to have the job done.)

THE PERFECTIONIST PROCRASTINATOR

Tom Peters and Robert Waterman brought us in touch with quality performance when they wrote the book *In Serach of Excellence.* On the front cover they proclaimed that here were lessons from America's finest and that implied that we could all learn the lessons. Now we'd have no excuse to be anything other than excellent. Here was everything we needed to know about excellent behavior.

This book has done a lot for procrastination. Before, we weren't really sure that perfection was possible. Now, unfortunately, we see in black and white that it is. How depressing. A vulnerable spot was hit when it was "discovered" that quality exists and there are people out there *doing* it...*right.* The only thing left to counterbalance this news is to reach for the one behavior that can bring us back some comfort: PROCRASTINATION.

Procrastination is an appealing strategy for dealing with all this "excellence stuff." Most of us are scared to death to be excellent. It might alienate us from our chums and co-workers. Remember the kid in fifth grade who always got the A's (maybe that was you?) Remember the teasing? And the name-calling?

Instead...mediocrity is comfortable...it feels like our old, well-worn pair of jeans. "Mediocrity" means "the quality or state of being normal." Mediocrity, as a word, has received a lot of bad press. Actually it seems a pretty comfortable place to be. If you've ever experienced excellence, it brought with it a certain pressure. Mediocrity, on the other hand, feels stable and like a cup of honey tea on a rainy winter day.

Excellence can be like trying to perform a water ballet in Niagra Falls. Even when the performance is over and you get the applause, part of you remembers being scared to death and you didn't enjoy it much. This survival mechanism wants to know if the applause was really worth it.

Procrastination offers a kindly hand in these circumstances. Put the task off long enough and either it isn't possible to do it at all OR it is only possible to do it in mediocre style. Not only are we off the hook to be excellent, we prove to ourselves that, given the proper amount of time, we *could have been excellent.* See, we managed to do *that much* in only a couple of (days), (hours), (minutes).

Besides, we all know what happens to some people who become excellent. They get egos like movie stars and temperaments like championship tennis players. They develop loud mouths like boxers and commercialitis like Olympic gold medal winners. They may even run for public office.

America is the only country that roots for the underdog and cannonizes its winners. America is probably the only place where *The Bible* and *Winning Through Intimidation* could share the best seller list.

We get mixed messages when the lyrics coming out of our AM radios are: "Be all that you can be" and then "Don't get above your raisin'." How to handle this confusion? Simple, procrastinate.

Procrastination allows us to believe that our ability is greater than what is seen in our performance. What you see is not necessarily what we can do.

Susan was a brilliant research analyst who was frequently introduced by her college credentials, Magna Cum from Ivy League. The offer from the nationally known research firm was absolutely expected and Susan began her corporate career. She had wrestled with procrastination in college and managed to do well with last minute Herculean efforts. Her professors did their part in encouraging her procrastination by extending due dates for important papers. (The education stage makes the best training ground for procrastinators. If you want to know how to procrastinate even better than you do now, sign up for a college course in anything and then practice your skill with the instructors. Some will participate in the game and show you how to get by with even less effort than you imagined possible. Many will actually help you avoid excellence altogether.)

Susan began to postpone the necessary interviews for her research assignments. She relied more on book statistics than face what felt to her like "cold calls." Although she looked busy and competent she would have sudden attacks of shyness that were really acts of procrastination. Her college awards hung on her office wall like neon lights that said: EXCELLENCE. Susan wanted her reports to be perfect but sooner or later she would feel overwhelmed with the assignments and she'd freeze.

"I wanted to be the very best at my work," said Susan. "I wanted to be better than the *partners*, even. But I spent more time with statistics and worrying about being the best. More than anything, I didn't want to disappoint myself."

Why would anyone who has been "excellent" and who wants so much to continue to be "excellent" suddenly turn to procrastination? Waiting 'til the eleventh hour and slamdunking a research project allowed Susan to see how well she could do under last-minute deadlines. It also allowed her to avoid being all that she believed that she could be. As long as she procrastinated, rushed a report that wasn't perfect, then she could allow herself to think that perfection, for her, was still possible. "If I had only had a little more time, I could be brilliant," she would say to herself.

Competence is really between our ears. And if we can say to ourselves, "I'm competent. I just didn't have enough time. If I had had the time, I could really show you how competent I can be" then we're off the hook. Susan was amazed at her ability to hand in work that was mediocre in the short time frames that she allowed herself. This only added to the procrastination habit. When asked about a perfect environment and a perfect time frame in which to work, Susan had to be honest..."I don't know what I'd do if I had everything I wanted in terms of work time and work place and then still handed in a less-than-perfect report. Then I'd really have let myself down."

Susan is a perfectionist. She has high standards about what makes for a perfect market analysis report. She is critical of her own work and the work of others. She knows excellence when she sees it. She can still hang onto the idea that she can produce excellent work (if she uses the art of procrastination).

I'll bet you thought that a perfectionist is a person who goes around *doing* things — like fluffing up the pillows on the couch, correcting grammar, compulsively removing invisible lint from lapels, polishing the Volvo and balancing checkbooks.

The truth is: I've never met anybody like this. I'd hire them in a minute, though, to do all that for me. This kind of person is, at least, *in the ballgame doing things.* The perfectionist that I am talking about is the person who says:

"There's a right answer and I have to find it."
"It has to be perfect."
"I'll wait until I can do it perfectly."

These people are *not* the over-achievers in life. Over-achievers are just people who have swung at the ball so many times that they've hit a few. And they keep swinging. They have a healthy view of perfection — they shoot for it and know that true perfection is never attainable.

Jon is a copywriter for a San Francisco advertising agency and he has been trying to write a novel. He has been a successful writer of ad copy for years and he is well paid by his top-notch creative firm. Writing has always been easy for Jon and he hasn't had to wait for inspiration. After nearly two years of procrastinating with his novel, however, he concluded that the distractions of personal relationships were the cause of his procrastinating. Jon severed ties with his current lady friend that ended a four-year relationship. He wrote social events out of his calendar in order to concentrate on his writing. He let his friends and relatives know that he was altering his lifestyle in order to work on the Great American Novel. After a month of celibacy and hermit life, a friend ventured to ask "How's the novel coming?"

"It's terrible. The pressure is terrific," said Jon. "I've created this great hole in my life so that I could do this thing. Unfortunately I *told* everybody about it. Now everybody expects me to perform. I have to come up with something or I'll look like a jerk. Harriet was understanding about breaking it off because I wanted to devote myself to this. If I don't write...she's going to be wondering what was really going on."

Jon had asked for and received the support of his girl friend, his co-workers, his family and friends. He created a situation where he felt that he had to be not only productive, but brilliant. "I have to do it perfectly," he said. "Everybody's counting on it." As a result, Jon couldn't get started.

"When my friend came to see me, I begged him to forget that I said I was going to write *anything*," Jon explained. "I told him to treat me like I was *really* ordinary and not trying to do something special. I realized then that I should have told everybody to leave me alone because I wanted to be alone...not because I was going to write anything. In fact, if I were honest, I suppose it was to end it with Harriet. I used the novel as an excuse. It worked...for awhile. Until I tried to write and my own perfectionist values got in the way."

Jon was the fifth child in a family of seven. "I was never expected to amount to much," he said. Jon excelled in school and with his writing career *without the expectations* of his parents or his teachers. Jon's natural state for being creative is when it is least expected. "If no one's looking, I can do it," Jon says. By telling everyone, including the defunct Harriet, that he had plans for greatness, Jon tied himself up in a knot that logically led to procrastination. "You know, once I decided to write the less-than-perfect book...and after I told a few people that I was really just ordinary...*then* I began writing."

The greatest number of perfectionists are *not* actually doing anything. They are sitting on the sidelines, suited up ready to play...and not playing.

That pretty much sums up this procrastinator style.

When I was ten years old, sitting on my Aunt Grace's piano bench, I was frozen with indecision about the next note to play. Eighty-eight black and white keys loomed before me like Hoover Dam and I was somehow supposed to know the right key to touch. My Aunt Grace taught piano at a Kansas college and every summer I lived with her and "studied music." Actually what I studied was procrastination. I learned to procrastinate for nine months every year and then practice eight hours a day memorizing a classical piece to play for her. There I sat — my thin, competent, talented aunt sitting ramrod straight beside me waiting, waiting for the next note to be played. Nothing came.

Finally in great desperation she spoke, "Do anything! Even if it's wrong!"

Well, she couldn't have said anything better to me. I credit my Aunt Grace with curing me of one brand of procrastination in one stroke. The silence at that piano bench was so long and so awful that *anything* was preferable to it.

Call this: Analysis Paralysis.

If I think that I have to do it perfectly, then I can't do it at all. I will freeze in front of the Piano Keys of Life. I still hear her voice when I get clutched with excellence: "Do anything! Even it it's wrong!"

A perfectionist puts unreal demands on their performance and then, like Jon, strives for the unobtainable and resorts to procrastinating. Sometimes it may be difficult to recognize a perfectionist who is procrastinating because they always seem to look like they're only in it half way. Inside, when self-esteem and anxiety get mixed into the same pot, the perfectionistic procrastinator will think:

1. "This should be easy for me." (After all, Jon was a successful writer...writing a novel should come easy.)

2. "I expect myself to come up with the right answer...and it'll be here in just a minute. And it will be perfect."

3. "I've performed perfectly in the past and I can expect myself to do this task alone and perfectly now." (Never mind that this is a difficult task.)

4. "If this isn't right, then everybody will know it." (So what if they do?)

While my daughter Kelly was attending the University of Oregon, she wrote an article for the school newspaper. She sent the article to me before submitting it to the newspaper. I read it and thought it was a funny article; I laughed at all the appropriate times. She asked for my opinion and I gave her a couple of suggestions, but it was basically ready for submission.

One month later, I asked her about the article. She hadn't sent it in. My initial response was, "What?! That was a good article!" And her predictable reaction was, "Well, I just didn't know if it was good enough."

("Okay, here it is," I said to myself. "You're looking right at a perfectionistic procrastinator at work. What are you going to say next?")

Kelly's shoulders were still in the shrug position when I started my spiel.

"You know what will probably happen if you send that article in...?" I began. "The newspaper staff, after they've finished shredding it and holding their noses, will send it to the journalism department. The head journalism prof will have copies made and passed around to all classes. And they'll say to every journalism student, 'Don't ever hand any drivel into us like this. Anybody caught writing anything this bad will be transferred to California.' They'll use your article as a standard of truly bad writing for years to come. It may even be reprinted in journalism textbooks as an example of poor taste. You'll be famous as the tackiest writer ever to hit a college campus and people will laugh and snigger at you on the street. There will be such a 'to do' about it that you won't know how to handle such attention.''

Kelly was laughing, of course, at this point and I concluded:

"You'll be a complete embarrassment to the whole family."*

After that, we dropped the subject of the article. One month later I got a "thank you" card in the mail and the recent issue of the university's newspaper with the published article in it...virtually unedited.

The perfectionist asks, "What if I give it my all and it fails?" Procrastination keeps us from giving it our "all." And when we don't give it our all, we have an excuse about why it isn't perfect. As perfectionists, we can be scared to death to get committed to a project, a relationship and/or responsibility of any kind. "If I can't do it perfectly, I don't want to try to do it at all." If our report, or idea, or artwork or craftsmanship is rejected, it would kill us...if we had tried our *best*. So we give it

*for a more complete description of this phenomenon, read *Making Things Better by Making Them Worse*, by Allen Fay.

second best, via procrastination. Then we're covered either way — if it's a hit, we can say, "Look what I did with one arm tied behind me," and if it misses, we can say, "Ah, well, what can you expect; I didn't really put my best effort into it anyway..."

Of all the procrastination characters, the perfectionist pays the highest price. Although procrastination keeps us safe, we're not really experiencing serenity. What could get you to take a flying leap into Life and make a commitment to that project?

How about: DON'T DIE WONDERING.

The price that we pay for the security of mediocrity is always wondering if we could have made it. That's a high price. And you may be at a point of time in your life when the price is too high.

James Sherman writes in his book *Do It!*, "There is no way procrastination can be eliminated until risk is accepted as a natural part of life."

It's a risk to do something well. It is a risk to do something as well as we can do it. It's risky business to put ourselves out there and reach for excellence. After all, it might not be seen as excellent by anybody else.

Is that really terribly important? As an artist, if you waited for the taste of the American public to find your work, you may have a long wait.

Procrastination may be robbing you of your potential. Is it time for you to steal it back?

Jerry asked Alice to make a shirt for him. Alice was a creative seamstress and appliqued elaborate patterns with colorful fabric. Jerry performed in a country western band on weekends and wanted the shirt to wear when he performed. He told the other band members, in front of Alice, about the wonderful work that she did and how perfect his shirt would be. Then he waited. For weeks. Alice procrastinated until Jerry forgot about the shirt. "I was so relieved when he stopped asking about it," said Alice. "I didn't want to risk trying to live up to his expectations."

So what's the worst that could happen?

"The shirt would be dumb-looking or wouldn't fit."

"And then?"

"I'd do another one or make the alterations to make it fit."

"What if he really hated the shirt?"

"Well, knowing Jerry...the worst that would happen would be that he'd hang the shirt up in his closet and forget about it."

"He wouldn't take out a full page ad in the local newspaper proclaiming your incompetence?"

(Laughter.) "No!"

What keeps the perfectionist procrastinator from getting in gear is: FEAR. What they don't realize is... everybody else is fearful too.

"There is nothing in this world that's worth doing that isn't going to scare you," writes Barbara Sher in *Wishcraft, How to Get What You Really Want.*

I agree. I always suspected that I was not the only fearful one. Each day is a chance to fail.

This reminds me of summer mornings on my grandmother's farm in Kansas. I was six years old and I wanted to watch my uncle milk the cows. And I was so afraid of the big, mooing animals that I couldn't get near the barn. "They're more afraid of you than you are of them," my uncle kept insisting. Finally after three or four summers of this, I ventured down to the barn and out into the corral. Each bovine outweighed me by a couple of hundred pounds. I started to walk towards them. Their big brown eyes rolled back into their heads until the suspicious whites showed. They arched their necks and bellowed in fear. They backed away from me and cried for my uncle to save them.

Most situations in life are like those cows. The situation may outweigh us... but things are usually more frightened and unsure of us than we imagine. If we start to walk toward the situation, often we'll catch the whites of their scared eyes as they move away from us.

This is a classic story about Sir Henry Morton Stanley, the 19th Century British explorer.

"After fighting his way through this incredibly horrifying jungle, he was asked if he'd been frightened. 'I didn't think about it that way,' he said, 'I did not raise my head to see the whole. I saw only this rock ahead of me. I saw only this poisonous snake in front of me that I had to kill to take the next step. Only after I had gotten through did I look back and see what I had been through. Had I taken a look at the whole thing, I would have been so scared that I would never have attempted this.' "

As a perfectionist you've been using procrastination to keep yourself from going out on a limb. That's understandable. Maybe you're looking at the whole when you only need to see the first part. Don't you ever wonder about what the possibilities would be if you just cut loose and did it?

I know a woman who lost over 100 pounds in less than a year. (The surprising thing is, she kept it off.) I asked her how she managed this almost impossible task and she said, "I didn't really think about losing 100 pounds. I just lost five pounds and I thought, well, that was okay, I think I'll see if I can lose five more...and I just kept that up. I never did lose 100 pounds in my mind. I lost five pounds *twenty times!*"

Barbara Sher writes: "Great deeds are made up of small, steady actions, and it is these that you must learn to value and sustain."

A perfectionist is typically impatient and wants it all — complete and perfect, right now.

Perfectionists expect a lot from themselves. And from those around them. We hear things like, "Practice makes perfect," and we assume that we have practiced enough so that whatever we do should be perfect. And rather than practice at anything, we freeze, put it off and then put up with the consequences. For some of us that means never beginning anything new. For others it means accepting mediocrity when we think we're capable of more.

Babe Ruth sums it up: "You can't hit 'em if you don't swing at 'em."

THE PAY VALUE: for the Perfectionist Procrastinator is never having to say you're sorry...because you don't ever risk doing anything unless you can do it perfectly.

THE PRESCRIPTION: for the Perfectionist Procrastinator is giving permission to one's self to do "it" imperfectly.

Identifying Self-Talk of the Perfectionist Procrastinator

"This has got to be right."

"I hope no one finds out."

"I want this to be perfect."

"I'm good at this. This *should* be easy!"

"Anything worth doing is worth doing well."
   (or perfectly)

"I can't afford a screw up."

"There is a *right way* to do this."

"If I do this right, they're going to expect everything I do to be perfect."

"I don't think I could stand it if I gave it my all and it failed."

"I could have done a lot better if I had had more time."

"Boy, I pulled this one off...imagine how good it could have been if I'd taken more time."

WALL MOTTOS
FOR PERFECTIONIST PROCRASTINATORS

(Post in convenient place. For greater effect, recite daily *aloud*. Replace your current Self-Talk with...)

"There is nothing in this world worth doing that isn't going to scare you."
—*Barbara Sher in* <u>Wishcraft</u>

"If you're not failing occasionally, then you're not reaching out as far as you can."
—*Nolan Bushnell in* <u>A Whack On The Side Of The Head</u> *by Roger von Oech*

"The way to succeed is to double your failure rate."
—*Thomas J. Watson*

"We can no longer wait around for the ideal opportunity. If we have not achieved our early dream, we must either find new ones or see what we can salvage from the old."
—*Rosalynn Carter*

AFFIRMATIONS

I am my own audience. I enjoy myself.

I deserve to complete projects.

It is okay to get dirty.

I am loved when I try new things.

Things don't have to be perfect. Things have to get done.

So what's the worst that could happen?

I release my Quality Control Director.

COMBAT TACTICS
FOR PERFECTIONIST PROCRASTINATOR

If you have identified yourself as a possible Perfectionist Procrastinator, do the following:

1. Ask yourself: what is the worst that could happen? What would happen if you took your time and put your heart into it and it wasn't perfect? What would really happen? Write the worst-case scene. Then go even further — assign yourself the task of doing it IMPERFECTLY. Make yourself do something...anything...less than perfect.

2. Ask yourself: What would the perfect time frame be for this and what would my perfect environment be for this? List in great detail what it would take for you to be perfectly at ease with this task...the right lighting, all your bills paid, every member of your family healthy, the dog fed, etc. Then take a good look at your list. You will come to this conclusion: there will never exist a perfect time and a perfect place for you to do this task. So do it anyway.

3. AN EXCELLENT CURE FOR PERFECTIONIST & LIST WRITERS!

Every day, ask yourself: what is the *one thing* I want to get done today? Perfectionists give themselves an impossible amount of work to do with impossible standards. The cure for this obnoxious inner chaos is to "chunk down" a task. At the end of the day, what was the *one thing* that you did that was your ONE THING? Start now. For tomorrow, what's your ONE THING task?

4. Practice looking ridiculous. That's right. Part of your nature dictates that you look "hip-slick-and-cool" all of the time. Gotta look good, no matter what. You've long since forgotten *why* or what would happen if you didn't. A perfectionist is constantly asking: How am I doing? The prescription for the perfectionist is to act imperfectly. Once you feel yourself act in an imperfect way, you'll see that it isn't the devastating experience that you thought it would be. A perfect place to get rid of your perfectionistic behavior is in an improvisational acting class. Once a week you'll be expected to make a complete fool of yourself. And that's just what you need. Because the rest of the week you'll look terrific by comparison. Find an outlet for acting imperfectly. Find something that you won't be expected to do perfectly. Then go do it imperfectly and see how it feels. Do it now.

"Eat a live toad every morning and nothing worse will happen to you the rest of the day."

5. One perfectionist kept a pair of shoelaces tied to her desk as a constant reminder: "I didn't know how to tie shoelaces perfectly the first time I tried that *either*."

Every time she saw the shoelaces, they gave her courage to try new things. You don't have to do it perfectly the first time; you just have to do it.

THE CRAZYMAKING PROCRASTINATOR

"His procrastination is driving me crazy."

The story you are about to read is absolutely true...nuts, but true.

"Ben and I had been married for three years when our refrigerator broke down. I suppose that doesn't sound like such a big deal...it's just that he said that he would handle it. Well, when Ben says it's his to do, three things fall into place:

1. I can't bug him about it.

2. I can't take over the job myself.

3. I can't hire anybody to do it either.

"So there we were without refrigeration for nearly three months. I'm not kidding. In total frustration, I did the only thing I could think of to do...I bought a small, cube-type, under-the-bar refrigerator that would hold a dozen eggs and some milk for the kids. I couldn't believe it! Three months without a refrigerator! Finally Ben got a repairman to look at the refrigerator. He fixed it with an $11.00 part. I'm telling you...Ben's procrastination is going to drive me CRAZY!"

Crazymaking procrastination is one of the most fascinating behaviors in the study of sabotage. It takes at least two players but many more can be involved. The stakes are anything from refrigerating your food to completing large architectural projects. The amount of irritation possible is incalculable and the length of play can be *years*. All it takes to play the game is a sincere desire to drive someone else really crazy. Procrastination is the perfect tool. Bosses can play it with employees but employees can play it back on their bosses. Spousal play is very popular. Parents and children can take turns playing it. Friends have been known to play it only for a little while and then just cease being friends...so the game won't last as long. People frequently encourage play even when they don't want to play any longer.

Why on earth would anybody want to drive you crazy?

Why, indeed. The reasons are as varied as the people who are engaged in this type of procrastination. Maybe they're just scared and you are the innocent bystander in their scheme of the world. Or maybe it's more entertaining to watch you get excited as deadlines loom large. Maybe it's a power struggle. Maybe you're on the receiving end of infantile rebellion.

In this type of procrastination the goal is to drive someone else crazy. For whatever reason. And it works.

"I was already married when I met Ann. It was a dead-end marriage and Ann was everything I had ever dreamed of," said Keith, a trial attorney. "I know that probably every man says this sort of thing, but Ann was incredibly special and she had a very special spiritual way of looking at the world. I lost no time in ending my marriage and marrying Ann. I had the most desperate feeling that I would not be able to live up to my potential until I could live with Ann. Her self-confidence and love of life was absolutely infectious. I had had nearly 35 years of being an obedient and responsible son, student and husband and lawyer. Ann represented Life on Planet Earth and I wanted to learn from her.

"After nearly a year together, I hadn't learned as much as I guess I thought I should. Ann still had what she had but I was no closer to adopting her way of seeing the world. It was the first time that I couldn't seem to grasp something. We went to human potential type seminars and we meditated together and we went on long walks together. Just when I thought that I had *the* answer, I'd realize that I didn't have a damned thing.

"I began to resent Ann. And I began to procrastinate about everything. I didn't pay the bills, even though that was my job. I promised to do things and then I'd never get to them. Of course, I didn't know all this at the time but I know it now.

"How could I be angry at Ann? I thought that she had THE answer, only to find out that there was no THE answer. That's the answer. So I planned trips and 'forgot' to make reservations. I let jobs around the house just go undone. I would start a project and then never finish it. Once I promised to work on an antique table she had brought home. I said that I would strip the thing for her. I got all the goop on it all right and then I just kind of hosed it down leaving part of the peeling gunk stuck to the table. I promised to finish it some day. I never did. After the divorce, she finished it."

Keith reached for one of the most effective tools to drive someone crazy. Ann responded perfectly.

Whether or not you are a procrastinator (and who isn't?), you may have to live with or near a procrastinator. Or you may have to work with one. Trying to deal with your own procrastination is bad enough...now trying to deal with someone else's may feel overwhelming. You may be living with a crazymaking procrastinator and not even realize it.

"He's such a nice guy," said Ann about Keith. "I had no idea of what was going on. Sure, he'd forget to pay the bills. And he was so busy with his work that he'd have to let some of the work around the house go..."

Dear, sweet, spiritual Ann. Ann had Keith on a pedestal...he could do no wrong. And he *didn't* do anything wrong. He didn't do *anything*, and that was the problem. Ann was forgiving. Far too forgiving, actually. Keith went to extreme measures to finally drive Ann crazy. Ann made up more excuses for Keith's behavior than Keith did. When Ann found that the electricity had been shut off for the fourth time in their townhouse, that was the last straw.

For anyone who is efficient and punctual, it is a frustrating experience being around a chronic procrastinator. They're late, they don't follow through on promises, they "forget" and often don't handle money well. If your financial future is tied into one of these exasperating individuals, you have plenty of company.

And if you try to help or take over a task, you can count on a fight. They will set up a circumstance, appeal to you for rescue and then be humiliated if you succeed. It's a perfect Catch-22 and makes for the best crazy-making material around.

The program chairperson for a professional organization called me one afternoon and requested that I give a luncheon speech at their March meeting. She specified the subject: procrastination. The audience would be primarily architects and engineers, she explained. After I got all the particulars about the meeting, I began asking Linda questions about the topic and what she would like to have covered. It didn't take long to discover it. "I want you to address specifically, how to deal with a procrastinating boss. The principals of our architectural firm drive the staff crazy with their procrastinating!"

I went to work on a speech that would give practical ideas for successful communication with bosses who were procrastinators. I learned that the strategies would be successful with married couples and family members as well. Trying to communicate with a superior in a work environment posed probably the toughest of the procrastinating challenges. Many people:

a) don't realize that they're procrastinating.

b) don't know that it is affecting others.

c) don't know how to behave any other way.

d) have been trained into procrastinating by their employees.

Notice that I did not say...they don't care. People do care...they care very much...about how they are being perceived and a boss, especially the owner of the firm, does not like to feel that they are actually the obstacle in the staff's work day.

It is appropriate here to talk about training. Not the kind you sign up for, either. People inadvertently train each other every day. If you are telling me a story and I lean forward as you tell it, and I nod my head in understanding and I ask you questions as you go along, you learn to tell stories to me, your waiting audience. If, instead, I gaze out the window and give you no reply, you take this as a communication punishment and you don't tell me stories.

Think about it... Don't you have a friend that you have lunch with that you already know what you're going to talk about? And you have another friend who, when you get together, you talk about completely different subjects? How do you know *who* to talk to about *what*? Your friends have trained you...with subtle, non-verbal and sometimes verbal cues of what they find interesting. You're trained. And so are your friends.

Chances are very good that you helped train the procrastinator in your life.

First take a look at your own behavior and see if there is anything there that could be considered "enabling" behavior. "Enabling" behavior is anything that enables the procrastinator to continue his or her procrastination. Or encourages it.

For instance...

Years ago I managed a printing department for an engineering firm. We had our share of rush jobs and that is the nature of printing. I always maintained the perspective, however, that printing is not a life and death matter. We weren't in the medical profession and no matter how hard the engineers tried, I knew that they really weren't going to die if the work didn't get done.

Well, engineers are creative folks and I noticed a couple of them bringing especially high priority work in on very short time frames. One day I watched as an engineer brought a proposal to the lead pressman. The engineer was excited and tried to impress the printer about the vital nature of the project. The entire future of the firm was resting with that one document, he would have the printer believe. I watched the printer carefully. He also got very excited, put the title of the project at the top of the scheduling board and immediately put the job into production with the platemaker. The deadline was met with much stress.

About a week later, the same engineer returned, this time with an even more important project. I watched as the pressman again mirrored the engineer's tense state and put the project into production. By day's end, the whole shop was again in an uproar and the work was done with much excitement. This time I watched the printer as he drove away from the building, headed for home. He looked exhausted. I looked at the proposal and I tallied the number of pages that went into the document. It wasn't an outstanding number. It wasn't any more pages than the printer would have done on any normal production day.

The excitement may have been fun for awhile but I did not want it to continue. I briefed the printers and the platemaker. "Accept the work," I said, "but don't accept the trauma."

The printer was *inadvertently* accepting stress from the engineer along with the pages to be produced. Every time the engineer brought in a project, he could count on the printer to share his dilemma with him. The printer would get excited, show his concern to the engineer and basically train the engineer to return with an even greater problem to solve. The engineer was only too happy to oblige. The engineer was receiving applause for his act: he could procrastinate with his project and then take it to printing and be treated like a very important person with a very important project.

V. I. P.
Very Important Procrastinator

If you are an employee with a procrastinating boss, the first thing you should look at is your own behavior. Have you inadvertently trained your boss to leave things to the last minute? How do you react to your boss's crises? Imagine that you can see yourself as your boss sees you. Do you somehow reward your boss (or your spouse) when they procrastinate?

Once the printer was told, "Accept the work. Don't accept the trauma," the scene in the pressroom changed. The engineer was visibly surprised when the printer simply accepted the pages to be printed, put them on the counter and continued his job on the press. The engineer repeated his plea and his plight and the printer nodded his understanding. The engineer flapped and talked some more. The printer said, "No problem. It'll get done." The engineer didn't believe him and wanted better service. He called for the manager...me. I listened and nodded too. I had to repeat his instructions back to him before he would believe that I comprehended the seriousness of his request. Eventually we had this engineer trained to treat printers with the same courtesy that any printer deserves. And the printer learned how to have a little bit more control over an already stressful job.

If you live with a husband or wife or child who continually procrastinates, have you inadvertently encouraged this behavior? Did you give plenty of attention to their procrastinating? Did you try a rescue? Did you tell them that it was okay after all, you understand? Did you nag or demand? Did you just simply give up and do it yourself?

Then you're asking for it. Count on more crazymaking procrastination because you're making it too much fun to quit the game now.

Crazymaking procrastination is one of the surest ways to resist domination. It's an expression that says, "I'm in control here." Ben, for instance, had complete control of the kitchen by procrastinating about the refrigerator. Children can rely on procrastination to voice their independence. It is a perfect way to "fight" without exchanging blows. "I'll do it when I'm good and ready," says the crazymaking procrastinator and that may be to the detriment of themselves as well as the people around them. A child might use procrastination to get noticed when there doesn't seem to be any other way to get it.

Procrastination can be the tip of a very ugly iceberg. When you are living in the situation, it may be a hard call to make. "It's hard to see the picture when you're part of the frame." The message of the procrastination may be coming through loud and clear...but you never hear the words.

THE PAY VALUE: for the Crazymaking Procrastinator is the opportunity to drive people crazy.

THE PRESCRIPTION: for the Crazymaking Procrastinator is to get honest about what relationships you want in your life and about what relationships you *don't* want in your life.

IDENTIFYING SELF-TALK OF CRAZYMAKING PROCRASTINATION

"I'll show them."

"Don't bug me."

"Get off my back."

"I'll do it. Just leave me alone."

"I said, I'll do it."

"Don't you trust me?"

"Well, you're not so perfect yourself!"

"So, let's see you do any better."

"Don't tell me what to do."

"If you're so smart, why don't you do it?"

"I'll get around to it."

WALL MOTTOS
FOR CRAZYMAKING PROCRASTINATORS

(Post in convenient place. For greater effect, recite daily *aloud*. Replace your current Self-Talk with...)

"Habit is habit, and not to be flung out the window...but coaxed down the stairs a step at a time."
—*Mark Twain*

"The shortest distance between two points is a straight line...don't sabotage me, *tell* me."
—*Z. Bohachi*

"The strong silent types are committing axe murders of silence."
—*Alyce P. Cornyn-Selby*

"You will know them by their actions."
—*Biblical saying*

AFFIRMATIONS

I attract honesty to myself.

I can respond honestly.

I deserve to be listened to.

It is okay to express displeasure.

I can talk to people about what I dislike.

I am not expected to like everything and everybody.

I am a person who will honor my commitments.

COMBAT TACTICS FOR CRAZYMAKING PROCRASTINATORS

If you have identified yourself as a Crazymaking Procrastinator, do the following:

1. Let me know who you are immediately so that I can avoid you and your crazymaking.

2. If you don't want to do a task, don't say that you'll do it. Develop your honesty muscles.

3. Have the good graces to hand the job over to someone who wants to have it done more than you do.

4. If there is some doubt in your mind, ask your surrounding human beings how your behavior is affecting them. "I seem to put things off more than I'd like to...do you notice this and if you do, does it make any difference to you?"

5. Ask for help. the following is a description of Goal Call, the only trademarked system for effectively dealing with procrastination. Goal Call can be accomplished with a spouse, a friend, a child or a counselor. A grocery store owner used his banker as his Goal Call buddy when he was trying to write the business plan for his store.

"We're going out for bid on our biggest job ever in six months. I have to have everything on-line in a timely manner. How will we ever make it?"

"I've just been given the most significant assignment of my career and it will take a year to complete. My usual method of operating is to leave everything to the last minute and then try and save myself. I just can't afford to do that this time."

"I desperately need to develop a marketing plan for my business and I just keep putting it off. It's essential...and yet...I'm so busy putting out fires. And I hate to write."

What is GOAL CALL?

> A means of gaining a goal without losing your mind.
>
> An organized method to minimize or control procrastination.
>
> A business plan *in action*...and documented.

How does GOAL CALL work?

> First: A one hour personal consultation session to establish the projection (goal) and answer the questions — where do you want to be? How will you know when you're successful?
>
> Second: A weekly phone call at a scheduled afternoon time (usually 10 minutes) and a verbal report from you on your progress.
>
> Then: A monthly report written and sent to you documenting and tracking the trail to the goal. Reinforcement commentary. Positive feedback and alternative plans.

Practice GOAL CALL with a friend, business associate, financial or marketing advisor...or hire someone, a writer perhaps, to give you that ever important monthly progress report.

Who needs GOAL CALL?

You do...

...if you work on projects with deadlines.

...if you own your own business.

...if you are preparing to start a new venture.

...if you have a goal that means a lot to you.

Results:

Projects and performance tracked.

Immediate feedback.

Written, documented report of your accomplishments.

Goal setting managed.

Mental worry tapes curtailed.

Training towards personal cure for procrastination.

Self-sabotage minimized or eliminated.

Discipline without pain.

Weekly consultation.

HOW MUCH MONEY, TIME AND ENERGY HAVE YOU LOST TO PROCRASTINATION?

COMBAT TACTICS FOR LIVING WITH A CRAZYMAKING PROCRASTINATOR

If you have identified that you are existing in close proximity with a Crazymaking Procrastinator (boss, child, spouse, relative, etc.), do the following:

1. Ask yourself: is this annoying because they just don't do what they say they're going to do OR does this person's behavior have a direct affect on my life (work)?

    If your crazymaker talks to you about the many things that they would like to do and they never really follow up...so what? But if, on the other hand, their procrastination has a relationship to your security and your performance, that's another matter. Waiting for your boss to make a decision that will affect your projects, expecting a spouse to pay bills and counting on the procrastinator to *be there*, these are serious issues. First, determine what's important and what isn't.

2. Hit 'em with it.

>A. Pick a low pressure time. Don't wait until you're frazzled and they're under pressure. Wait until the crisis has passed. Set a time, a date and a place.
>
>B. Use "I" statements rather than "you" statements. Describe your relationship to them and how their procrastination is affecting you (and your performance, your comfort). "*I* can't give this project my best when the deadline runs out," is better than, "*You* put things off and screw things up." Describe *your* difficulty with the situation.
>
>C. Ask for their help in solving it. "I don't know what to do when this happens and I want you to tell me how I can handle this." (The miracle is that for some procrastinators, once they know they are causing a problem, they change their behavior.)
>
>D. Get your own agenda out on the table. "I am really committed to doing a good job and going for excellence when I can. In order to do that I need help from you."
>
>E. Be specific about what change you want. Simply saying, "I want you to stop procrastinating," is not good enough. The wording needs to be in proactive, positive terms. "Let me know the decision by Wednesday afternoon and I can deliver the report in seven days." "Pay each bill within 30 days or ask me to help you with it."
>
>F. Don't set the crazymaking procrastinator up. "Here are six things to do on your way home from work tonight."

3. Last ditch efforts.

   If your crazymaking procrastinator won't listen or you don't have a comfortable relationship with him or her, then contemplate the following:

   A. Get smart. Watch for predictable patterns and anticipate problems before they occur. Chances are *very* good that you already know the usual crisis situations. Have a healthy respect for your own sanity. Roll with the punches.

   B. Nail 'em. For anything that directly involves you, press for specific information. WHEN YOU REALLY LISTEN TO PEOPLE SPEAK YOU WILL BE AMAZED AT HOW OFTEN QUESTIONS *DO NOT GET ANSWERED*. Keep asking your question until you do get an answer. Watch your tone of voice and reword the question if you have to, just get the answer to your specific question.

   C. Get the overall. Ask your crazymaking procrastinator to describe the overall — the whole scheme to you — and often they figure out for themselves that it isn't possible or realistic to do the work in that amount of time. "What's the deadline and what is involved in this...I'm not sure I understand..."

D. Find the fear factor. If you suspect that this person is acting this way because of fear, then try the old "making it better by making it worse" gambit. Paint a picture for them of the worst-case scene. After a good laugh, see if the log jam doesn't start to move. "If an issue of this magazine ever comes out on time," the production manager said to the editor, "subscribers probably won't recognize it...or they'll all have heart attacks. Then we'd be sued, go bankrupt and lose our jobs. How's our insurance, anyway?"

E. Reward the person with good words (pat on the back, handwritten note) when they honor a commitment or finish a task.

F. Let it fail. Don't meet the deadline. You always pull it out of the fire. What would happen if you didn't? What would your crazymaking procrastinator learn from this experience?

G. Set your limits. Can you tolerate this person's behavior much longer? Is your serenity and productivity royally disturbed because of this person's procrastinating? Set limits on how much you are willing to put up with...perhaps there are other redeeming values...and if there aren't, examine the possibility of living without the irritation all together. Leave.

THE "NICE" PROCRASTINATOR

We've talked about some pretty tacky procrastinators, now it's time to see if procrastination can't be used for something "nice."

Ned was a friendly, well-liked accountant in a public works department. He always remembered birthdays at the office and frequently brought rolls for coffee break. Cute kid pictures of his children lined the shelf behind his desk. Ned could be counted on to volunteer to help with the staff picnic and he could tell a pretty good joke. Everyone seemed to like Ned and no one ever heard him say, "No."

Work did not progress through Ned's department well. Many of the staff signed up for sessions with the employee assistance counselor who began to notice a guilt pattern in several people. On the surface, the faces smiled in the corporate cubbyholes and the staff ate Ned's Danishes while they drank their coffee.

Behind his "niceness" Ned was well-guarded. He had the typical American fear of conflict in interpersonal relationships. His "nice" guy behavior provided him with a path of the least resistance. The people who worked for Ned knew of his "niceness" and no one could really dare to complain about Ned's chronic procrastination.

Ned had an elegant gift for sincerity. His compliments were warm and specific. He was courteous and helpful. He was also a deadbeat when it came to deadlines. Ned was a masterful example of the Nice Procrastinator.

The guilt on the part of the staff was understandable. Since Ned was so "nice" then there must be something wrong with *them*. Ned's act was so complete that the people working for him would not criticize Ned to each other. To say something un-nice about such a "nice" guy would be heresy.

Ned felt a little out of his league in a public works department. There were public financial matters that he simply did not understand and this fear caused him to pause...and pause...and pause. Asking for help would have been to admit to his ignorance. Ned wasn't up for that. He procrastinated and his staff saved him. Repeatedly. And they seemed happy to do it. Happy to help out such a "nice" guy. It was a perfect system.

It was perfect until Juliet, his primary assistant, went on a month-long vacation to Africa. Juliet's chores were taken over by a temporary student intern from another city department. Sheila was efficient and unemotional. She didn't even notice that Ned was a "nice" guy. Sheila only saw tasks and numbers. Sheila was also fairly outspoken. Within three weeks the employee assistance counselor had to mediate a mutiny in Ned's department. Sheila had called a spade a spade and Ned's procrastination was exposed for what it was.

Procrastination is an excellent strategy when you don't want to be the bad guy and say "No." If you add to that a lot of nice guy behaviors — like compliments and rolls with the coffee — you can get away with murder for years. When you are presented with a task to do (that you don't want to do), simply accept it and then put it aside. Look busy most of the time, but always be cheerful. Smile a lot. Teeth are a sure sign of a Nice Procrastinator.

Why do you suppose this works so well?

When was the last time you thanked someone for saying "no" to a task?

We do not reward honest, up front behavior, that's why the Nice Procrastinator exists. That's it in a nutshell.

Give a project to a Nice Procrastinator and they will gladly accept it and behind that smiling face is a "no." Only they don't say "no." They are *counting* on you to be a nice person and not ream them out for procrastinating. And you usually don't. You grind your teeth and walk away while they are still flashing their teeth. There's a lot of teeth showing in this system. But not everyone is happy.

Now give the project to someone who is not so nice and they too, do not want to do it. They tell you so. Sometimes they're polite and sometimes they're not. But at least they tell you "no."

WHAT DO YOU DO NEXT?

Do you take your project and thank this person for saying "no"? No way. We do not reward the honesty and their assertiveness. Since there is no reward for saying "no" then saying "yes" is a lot easier. And procrastinating about it is just as easy.

Let's talk about the Concept of "Badges."

Badges are the imaginary buttons that we wear on our lapels that tell *us and everyone else* who we are. They aren't literally there. But we imagine that we have *identifiers* that are important to us. One badge may read: Good Parent. Another badge might say: Good Driver. Yours might say: Good Employee.

These badges are critically important to us and we suffer extreme feelings when dirt is thrown on our badges. Anything that implies that you are *not* a good employee, when you have a badge that says "good employee," will cause emotional *trouble*.

My friend Marj called me one evening and she was very distressed. One of her neighbors had complained to her about her small son's behavior during sidewalk play. Marj could take the criticism for only so long before it began to wear away at her Motherhood Badge. By the time she had called me, she was in trouble with it. After about an hour, I said, "Oh, so that's it! You just had dirt thrown on your Motherhood Badge!"

The incident did not mean that Marj's Badge now reads: Bad Mother. It was clear that there was just a little dirt on the original badge. Once the mental image of the Motherhood Badge was restored, so was Marj's confidence level.

Many of us have a badge that reads: Nice Person. There is nothing wrong with this...unless it is more important to you than the badge that says: Honest Person. When "nice" is more important to you than "honest," then we have Nice Procrastinators. Procrastinating becomes the answer when we can't say "no."

THE PAY VALUE: for the Nice Procrastinator is the continued appearance of being "nice."

THE PRESCRIPTION: for the Nice Procrastinator is to find other ways of expressing "nice" behavior so that when the time comes, you won't be afraid to say "no."

IDENTIFYING SELF-TALK OF THE NICE PROCRASTINATOR

"Yes."

"Yes, of course."

"Why are they asking *me* to do this?"

"I am a soft touch."

"I just can't say 'no'."

"If I say 'no' then nobody will like me."

"It's not my fault."

"I can get by this time."

Do you frequently give little gifts or offer food to help get you off the hook when you procrastinate?

WALL MOTTOS
FOR NICE PROCRASTINATORS

(Post in a convenient place. For greater effect, recite daily *aloud*. Replace your current Self-Talk with...)

"I don't approve of my attitude."
—*Katherine Hepburn*

"Honesty is the best policy — there's less competition."
—*John Childress*

"If you try to please everybody, nobody will like it."
—*Anonymous*

"I don't want 'yes men' around me. I want people who will tell me the truth even though it costs them their jobs."
—*Samuel Goldwyn*

AFFIRMATIONS

People appreciate it when I please myself.

I have a right to my thoughts, opinions and refusals.

I am a courteous person.

Conflict is natural and I can handle conflict gracefully.

It is not what happens to me but how I handle it that determines my well being.

I am my own best friend.

COMBAT TACTICS FOR NICE PROCRASTINATORS

If you have identified yourself as a possible Nice Procrastinator, consider the following:

1. Practice saying "no" to little things...things that really don't matter that much to anyone else. "No, I won't be going by the post office today."

   Your assignment is to find *something* to say "no" to every day for a week. Keep track in a calendar book or notebook. How did you feel? What was the reaction? Were you punished or rewarded for saying "no"?

2. Make a pact with someone who will encourage you to say "no." Rewards in life may be long in coming if you don't *ask for them*. The fastest way to get better behavior from yourself is to instruct someone to give you a pat on the back when you do it right. Doing it right, for you, is saying "no" and actually getting rewarded for it.

3. Take a good course in assertiveness. You'll learn that saying "no" is not a crime. A class will give you a safe environment to practice assertiveness and saying "no".

4. Practice saying "thank you" when anyone says "no" to you. How are we ever going to get any further until we start saying "thank you"?

5. Find other ways of being nice to people. Be so nice to people that it won't matter when you finally say "no" to them. Be creative — how many ways can you find to be nice today?

"DON'T RELY ON ME" PROCRASTINATOR

"The only thing you can rely on," my friend said about his favorite aunt, "is her unreliability."

My friend loved and admired his Auntie Mame-type aunt who lived up in the pea fields country of Eastern Washington. This old lady still drove her 1952 Hudson wildly through the streets of Pullman. She made a reputation for herself as the most unpredictable eccentric north of the Snake River...a reputation that she worked at and cherished.

"The only way to raise children," said the crazy old aunt, "so that they don't restrict you...is to be as totally nuts as possible." She explained that, to her way of thinking, human relationships died of boredom and that expectations killed more marriages than any other factor. She spent a great deal of time and energy (and money!) making sure that no one knew exactly what to expect of *her*. Her nephew, my friend, admired his aunt and his face softened when he remembered her, telling stories of her antics.

Unfortunately, my friend tried to duplicate his aunt's reputation in a different way. He procrastinated to show his desire to be seen as unreliable. His results were not quite the same as his aunt's, but it did give me another character to write about...

Procrastination is an excellent tactic for those people who would just as soon be thought of as unreliable and undependable. Life is easier when you're not relied upon to do anything. And everyone is surprised and pleased when you do *anything*.

Frequently procrastination is used as a way of looking eccentric or in some way, just a little different. In the same way many artists feel that they must be messy, people desiring to be "different" may procrastinate. Artists can be well organized, clean and punctual. A flamboyant eccentric need not procrastinate.

The problem with being dependable is that people come to believe that you can be depended upon in all sorts of circumstances. It is a risk to assume that one area of competence automatically presumes another. If you are a *very* reliable person, you may get more attention and more demands on your time and energy than you are willing to accept. Who needs it? Life can get to be one big demand after another when you're the one who can be relied upon to get things done.

Listen to the "advantage of being inept."

"I make sure that everyone knows that I don't know how to cook," says one woman who has wrestled with a weight problem for years. "If I don't have to cook, I can keep myself under control with food. When it comes to potluck dinners, I volunteer to bring the napkins."

"I got tired of everyone expecting me to drive," said one teenage boy. "I just started talking like I really wasn't very good at it and my crowd found other means of transportation. I didn't like being used. Not all the time anyway."

"If I let my roommates know that I know what to do with a screwdriver, then I'll have to fix everything around here."

"One of the best excuses I ever had (for getting out of things) was having a business project in another town. Whenever something came along...I couldn't be depended upon to be here. It was terrific! People would begin their conversations with, 'I suppose you're going to be out of town...' "

"I could never rely on my mother to be where she said she was going to be. Now that I'm a mother, I can see what freedom there is in *not* being dependable. I'm very dependable and I feel like I'm constantly being used as a cab driver for my kids' activities. My mother never had that problem. Maybe Mom knew best after all..."

"People have finally given up on me because of my procrastination. I have worked a long time for this. The only problem is meeting anyone new who doesn't know me. I count on everyone else to clue them in...then I make sure I procrastinate just for their benefit for awhile. I can't stand the restriction on my personal freedom."

"If I do well now, the expectations will be that I should always do well. Nobody gives you the freedom to fail. We're all expected to be perfect. Now I am aware that I procrasatinate to such a great degree that I can't *possibly* do the job well. I don't *want* their expectations."

These are typical responses from people who have discovered the power of procrastination...and appearing somehow incompetent. They procrastinate for very good reasons. Life will somehow go smoothly, as long as they keep this up. And often they get just what they want.

"I just want people to leave me alone."

THE PAY VALUE: for the "Don't Rely on Me" Procrastinator is a sense of personal freedom.

THE PRESCRIPTION: for the "Don't Rely on Me" Procrastinator is an increase of solitude.

IDENTIFYING SELF-TALK OF THE "DON'T RELY ON ME" PROCRASTINATOR

"If they know what I can do, I'll never get any peace."

"Well, I'll try..."

"I don't know if I can..."

"What's going to happen next?"

"Why are they asking *me* to do this?"

"I'll fix *them*."

"How am I going to get out of this mess?"

"People expect too much from me."

"I wish they'd go away and leave me alone."

"One thing leads to another."

"A clean desk is the sign of a sick mind."

"It's always something."

WALL MOTTOS
FOR "DON'T RELY ON ME" PROCRASTINATORS

(Post in convenient place. For greater effect, recite daily *aloud*. Replace your current Self-Talk with...)

"I just want to be alone."
—*Greta Garbo*

"The happiest of all lives is a busy solitude."
—*Voltaire*

"I never found the companion that was so companionable as solitude."
—*Henry David Thoreau*

AFFIRMATIONS

I have a right to some alone time today.

My solitude is a gift that I give to myself.

I will only agree to what I can do.

I will give myself time to think today.

I will not say "yes" without thinking.

I am a reliable person.

I handle people and situations easily.

COMBAT TACTICS FOR "DON'T RELY ON ME" PROCRASTINATION

If you have identified yourself as a "Don't Rely on Me" Procrastinator, then consider the following:

1. Give yourself what the world won't give you: SOLITUDE. The message of your brand of procrastination is "Leave me alone and don't expect anything from me...don't even ask." If being alone is what you want, then being alone is what you should have.

   THE DESIRE FOR SOLITUDE IS THE PRIMARY CAUSE OF SELF-SABOTAGING BEHAVIOR.

   Every human being needs "alone time" like we need air and food and water. Some of us need a lot of it and some of us need very little...but we all need to be alone once in awhile. It is our *right* to be alone. Some of us get all the alone time we need when we drive to work in the morning. Many more of us, however, need gallons more solitude and we're not getting it.

   The cure for most self-sabotage and the prescription for the "Don't Rely on Me" Procrastinator is: do anything you have to do to spend more time by yourself.

   Your assignment: Spend one hour ALONE this next week that you wouldn't get ordinarily.

2. Develop the muscles in your face that are responsible for the words: "I DON'T WANT TO."

Understand that the bottom line response for any pressure is:

a) "I did it because I wanted to."

b) "I didn't do it because I didn't want to."

There's nothing more to argue after that. Take a look...

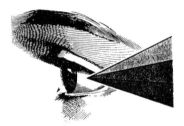

"Phyllis, why didn't you cook for the potluck?"

"Because I didn't want to."

OR

"Why don't you spend the weekend at the beach?"

"Because I don't want to."

Or try the flip side...

"Why did you see that awful horror film?"

"Because I wanted to."

OR

"Why did you buy a 1940 Ford?"

"Because I wanted to."

OR

"Why did you go out with *him*?"

"Because I wanted to."

See how it works?

Develop the jaw muscles that will allow you to say these key words. For help with your jaw, use your *backbone*.

3. If you're a "Don't Rely on Me" Procrastinator because you want to be perceived as some sort of eccentric, then express your eccentricity in some other way. Have a bowling alley installed in your living room. Raise llamas. Start your own mail order business. If your desire is to be some sort of likable oddball, then use something other than procrastination to get what you want.

THE FEELING GOOD PROCRASTINATOR

"Dear Alyce,

"I cannot begin to tell you...no, that's not right...I *am* going to tell you the *difference* that has suddenly happened in my life.

"There was one particular thing that you *said* that 'clicked' with me. It has changed my attitude, my self-talk and now my behavior. Co-workers have noticed the change. My family has commented on it.

"That one thing was: 'You don't have to like it, you just have to do it.'

"Before I really looked at my procrastination (which threatened both my job and my marriage), I seemed to have it in my head that I had a moral obligation to myself to feel good all the time. It was a reverse of the work ethic and I picked it up during the '60's when I heard: if it feels good, do it. I also heard: if it doesn't feel good, don't do it.

"I have avoided tasks that would take me outside of my comfort zone. It is not possible to be successful in sales and not be outside of your comfort zone most of the time. And weekends were the worst. I worked hard all week at my sales job. I used to feel that my weekends *had* to be used for leisure — NO MATTER WHAT — and that I had an obligation to myself to goof off even when there were things that I really wanted to do.

"I haven't turned into a workaholic. I have turned into someone who gets things done — even on weekends — and I do things that are distasteful, sort of, like cleaning off the top of my work bench. The miracle is...now that I have permission to be uncomfortable (and to *not* feel good), I actually feel more comfortable with my life. It is *enjoyable* to get things done and it's perfectly all right to not like the chore, just to do it.

"I don't know that I'm cured forever of procrastination but I like my life better.

"And I didn't procrastinate about writing this letter.

"Regards, Dave"

In a world of instant coffee, instant oatmeal, instant credit, direct dialing, drive thru banking, electric pencil sharpeners, high speed escalators and microwave ovens, it is pretty easy to see that we *like it easy*. And the easy way out often means procrastinating. We like to feel good. We put off doing things that don't feel good. That makes sense.

What doesn't make sense is putting off something that you say you really want because you feel that you have a *moral obligation to feel good all the time*. Just because you're not wallowing in pleasure doesn't mean that it isn't worth doing.

THE PAY VALUE: for the "Feeling Good" Procrastinator is upholding the moral obligation to "feel good."

THE PRESCRIPTION: for the "Feeling Good" Procrastinator is the realization that "you don't have to like it."

IDENTIFYING SELF-TALK OF THE FEELING GOOD PROCRASTINATOR

"This is a drag...should I really be doing this?"

"Are we having fun yet?"

"If it doesn't feel good, it must be punishment."

"If I put this off long enough, it might get to be fun."

"I'm a fascinating person; I don't deserve this."

"Where is the *joy*? Where are the *roses*?"

"If I were really smart, this would be easy."

"I'm not sure that I want to be caught *working*..."

WALL MOTTOS
FOR FEELING GOOD PROCRASTINATORS

(Post in convenient place. For greater effect, recite daily *aloud*. Replace your current Self-Talk with...)

"What have you got to win?"
—*Matthew Simek*

"The truth is that it just isn't human nature to feel good all the time."
—*Barbara Sher in her book "Wishcraft"*

"Success does not depend on how you feel."
—*Barbara Sher also from "Wishcraft"*

"No pain, no gain."
—*sports phrase*

AFFIRMATIONS

It is okay for me to be uncomfortable.

I do not *have to* feel good all the time.

It is okay for me to work hard.

I enjoy completing tasks.

I enjoy the process of work.

My work is fun for me.

COMBAT TACTICS FOR THE "FEELING GOOD" PROCRASTINATOR

If you have identified yourself as a Feeling Good Procrastinator consider the following:

1. Understand: You don't have to *like* it, you just have to *do* it. Everything from writing a query letter to an editor to making a cold call in a sales situation...it's uncomfortable and you're going to do it anyway. You don't have to baby yourself for the rest of your life — hasn't it been a drain on you to be constantly worrying about feeling good all the time? Has it *really* worked?

2. "No pain, no gain" is a tad extreme, but it makes the point. While cleaning the garage you may get your Nikes dirty, muss your manicure or deprive yourself of a few hours of television — TRUE — but the next time you need to use a wrench, you'll be able to find it and now you'll be able to park your Volvo *inside* the garage.

3. Incorporate the "feel good stuff" with the "I gotta do stuff." Here's how that works:

> I had been procrastinating about writing a script for a new client of mine — a college. Other things had come up so I felt justified as I shuffled my notes from one end of my desk to the other for more than a week. One Wednesday evening I found myself in the grocery store (food shopping is a task that I despise) and I realized that yep, I was indeed procrastinating about the script and I had stooped to the level of doing something I didn't even *like* to do. When I walked out to my car I was talking to myself about going home and getting serious about the script. A very strong voice inside of me said very clearly: "I don't want to." Great. Now what? So I asked myself: what do you really want to do right now?
>
> Well, it was a sweet, bright Oregon evening and I knew exactly what I wanted to do...I wanted to go for a drive. The car was well-tuned and full of gas and I said, okay, go driving.
>
> I hadn't made it the full length of Hawthorne Boulevard before an idea for the script started to come to me. By the time I had turned onto Morrison Street and headed for the Willamette River, I had composed the opening dialogue. I pulled into a parking lot and scratched out a few lines in a notebook in the front seat. As the Chevy and I glided out onto I-5 and circled northbound across the Fremont Bridge, chunks of the script fired in my brain. As easy as listening to the radio, I heard the narration for the project as I continued to drive. By the time I got home, all I had to do was type what I had heard.

Two days later the project was ready for the client. The college loved the script and we were ready to go to the sound studio with it.

By accident, I had learned a valuable lesson. By listening to the "still, small voice within" and foregoing the standard methods of scriptwriting (staring at paper in a typewriter), I got what I wanted — twice over.

When I stopped *trying* to write a script, the script arrived.

One of the most efficient things a Feeling Good Procrastinator can do is to incorporate a "feeling good" activity (in this case, driving) with an "I-gotta-do" activity (scriptwriting).

4. Wave the carrot in front of your nose.

"When I finish the dishes, I'll have a second cup of coffee."

"When I write three more pages, I'll go take a nap."

"Get the car washed, we'll all go for ice cream."

It's a technique as old as donkeys and carrots and it still works!

CHAPTER 4:
WHAT ARE MY OPTIONS?

There are lots of different ways to enjoy your stay on this planet. One of the tools of dealing with life is certainly PROCRASTINATION.

At any one time you may be several different procrastinators. You procrastinate for this benefit with this task and you procrastinate in this other area for a completely different reason.

The main message of the *Procrastinator's Success Kit* is: procrastination is an option.

Telling yourself to STOP PROCRASTINATING is a useless conversation. Beating ourselves up with internal lectures is annoying and offers no results. Self-help pep talks and time management are often of little help.

Recognize the benefit (or PAY VALUE) of your procrastination and then see if you can get the benefit without the use of procrastination. If you *did* stop procrastinating, you'd leave a hole in your life...and you'd wonder why.

There are so many things to do that it is unreasonable to expect yourself to do all of them. That means that you have to *not do* some of them. What you pick to *not do* is just as important as what you pick to *do*. We know this better at a subconscious level than at a conscious level.

What does that mean?

It means that you will say that you're going to do something. Consciously you really think that you might do it. Frequently we hear ourselves use language like:

> should do it...
> ought to do it...
> have to do it...
> must do it....

Subconsciously, in our heart of hearts, we know that we can't do everything. Knowing this, we select what we're going to do. What we select unconsciously to do has little connection with what we *say* we're going to do. In fact, the distance between words and actions is about 12 inches...between our heads and our hearts.

Procrastination is not the evil, laziness that you thought that it was. It is not a cruel joke that you play on yourself either. Instead, procrastination is an effective way to handle your stay on this planet. It *is* an option. You may be ready to try other ways, however, to living your life. Procrastination is a *choice* and it may be one that you're ready to stop using right now...knowing, of course, that you can pick it up again later.

Does this sound a little radical to you? I hope so. Because the conventional methods aren't working.

I hope you enjoyed this book. If you have any thoughts or comments or creative experiences you would like to share, I would be delighted to hear from you. Address all correspondence to:

Alyce P. Cornyn-Selby
c/o Beynch Press Publishing Company
1928 S.E. Ladd Avenue
Portland, Oregon 97214
503-232-0433

P.S. I highly recommend Barbara Sher's book *Wishcraft: How to Get What You Really Want* (Ballantine). Her step-by-step plan helped my dreams come true. I hope *your* dreams, whatever they are, will come true for you.

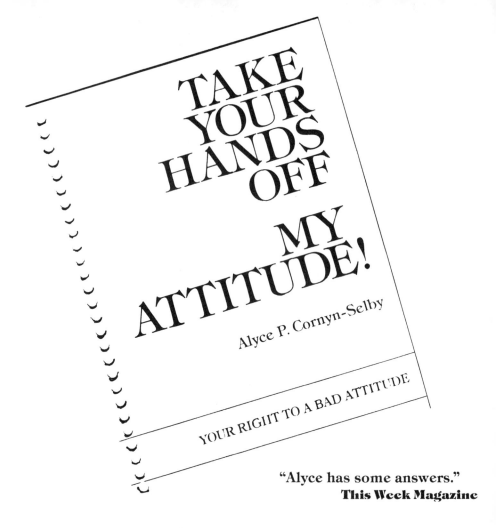

- An excellent book for employer/employee relationships and for parent/child relationships.
- Separates attitude from behavior.
- Learn to ask for AND GET behavioral changes.
- A Mega-Mini Book...big ideas in small packages.
- Can be read in less than 10 minutes.
- 4½" x 5½" handy size...you'll read it often!

Send $7.50 + $1.00 postage/handling to:
 Beynch Press Publishing Company
 1928 S.E. Ladd Avenue
 Portland, Oregon 97214

The INNER THEATRE MANUAL

A Step-By-Step Guide to Communicating With Your Internal Directors

"What internal directors?"

You know...the voices inside your head: THAT'S WHERE THE ACTION IS!

Your jury, your vice-presidents, the people inside of you...
    Your Financial Director: "You can't have that."
    Your PR Director: "Don't wear that."
    Your Health Director: "Lose weight. Exercise."
    Your Social Conscience: "This time, read the voters' pamphlet."
    Your Department of Environment: "Clean this place up!"
    Your Time Keeper: "Hurry up! You're late!"
You know what we mean--those voices that direct your life.

<u>These people are really in charge of your success.</u>

If you are considering a major purchase...
If you experience Writers Block...
If you are in the middle of a BIG DECISION...
If you are considering changing CAREERS...
If you are stuck in a procrastination...
If you have gained and lost and gained weight...
If you need to INFLUENCE YOURSELF...
If you can't understand why you say you want to do something and then don't do it...
  THIS is the step-by-step how-to communication system.

GOING TO THE INNER THEATRE

1. The setting.

Create a place in your imagination/mind where you will do your "work"--the work of processing dilemmas, questions, purchases, behavioral changes--anything from writer's block to purchasing a car to losing weight. This setting needs:
 a) comfortable spot for you--an overstuffed chair, a throne, whatever suits you.
 b) suitable access for about 200 "others". A theatre setting works well, a grandstand made of bleachers, a gynmasium, an elegant ball room.

2. The method.

3 ways to use this method:
 ...get quiet and *listen* to the dialogue.
 ...have a trusted friend or counsellor talk you thru a negotiation.
 ...write it.

Writing has the advantage of: you have a written record of the conversation and can go back over it; you will have a tendency to stay on track with the issue better if writing; writing has been known to improve health ("subjects who wrote about problems had an increase in white blood cell count and sensitivity"). Written dialogues will look like scripts.

Example
HD (Health Director): Buy a rowing machine. That's what we need!
FD (Financial Director): Are you nuts? They're expensive!
HD: Let's go to the discount place and check it out.
FD: TV advertises the cheap ones for $39.
HD: They don't look like they'd work.
FD: Is this going to be another one of your fads? I hate it when we buy something and then you don't use it!
HD: This time is different!
FD: Why don't we just walk around the block for exercise? The dog needs the exercise too.

And so it goes...

3. The process.

This is how to open a dialogue with an internal character. You need to get to the "right" one. Talking to a director who has no stake in the issue is like phoning a wrong number. Depending on what issue you chose, there will be some characters who are vitally interested in the issue and some that don't care about the issue.

You may experience a little "static on the line" at first if you try to contact an internal director who has been controlling an issue for you for a long time (such as weight). This internal person has a great deal of power and they are winning. Your initial feeling about this person may be: *boy, if I get my hands on 'em, I'm gonna kill 'em!*

This is not a great way to enter a negotiation. Don't go to the Internal Theatre with the attitude of kicking butt. These are your Survival Mechanisms and they have done a superior job of taking care of you. They have VERY GOOD REASONS for doing what they do. Trust this. You may at first believe that there can be no possible "good reason" for this sabotage (like the weight sabotage, for instance). Your task is to discover what the VERY GOOD REASON is.

Characters in your Inner Theatre may be male, female, animal, vegetable or mineral. They may appear as a ball of light. You don't have to direct this. There is no right or wrong experience here (where *else* can go for such a delightful time?). Your Financial Director does not have to wear a 3-piece suit. Your Health Director does not have to wear jogging shorts. Lighten up. *Take what you get.*

When you have your theatre pictured, say: I want to work on the issue of __X__ (fill in the blank). I want to speak to the person who is in charge of __X__. Would that person please stand up?

When the person (or entity) identifies her/himself,

THANK THEM.

"Thank you for identifying yourself. Would you be willing to speak with me about this issue?"

DO NOT ASK "WHY" QUESTIONS. Too often a "why" question is a thinly disguised judgement call. It's a pretty good idea to not ask or answer "why" questions *in or out* of the Inner Theatre. Instead, state your questions in a different way.

"Of what benefit are you to me?"
  OR
"You serve a good purpose in my life and I appreciate that. What good purpose do you serve?"
  OR
"You've been with me a long time. You must be very important. What pay value are you in my life?"

A Survival Mechanism is there for your *survival.* They feel protective of their mission. Protection against what? For every person who has extra weight on, for example, there's another reason to have it on. Your "very good reason" is as individual as you are. That's why there are no set formulas. You find your own way. "Life is a personal event."

4. Guidelines.

What do you do if you want to speak to a character (i.e. Fat Person) but they don't answer?

(This ain't AT&T. Pretent it's the European phone system and try again OR...do it in writing!)

Don't be surprised if you encounter resistance. This may be due to a variety of things--can't you guess at what they might be?

a) the "good reason" may be highly protected, very personal and the Survival Mechanism feels that you can't handle knowing what the "good reason" is.

b) the Survival Mechanism doesn't trust you. Is there any reason why they should? In order to get past this one, you may have to demonstrate your trustworthiness to another character first. For instance, make a commitment to your health or your finances, honor that commitment and the other directors will make note of it.

c) they don't want to talk to you because they think you're going to ridicule them or *try to talk them out of how they think or feel.*

5. Continuing the dialogue.

Cultivate the phrase "would you be willing?" These are the words of a skilled negotiator. Learn to negotiate peaceful settlements within yourself.
Examples:
"Would you be willing to work with me on this issue?"
"Would you be willing to take off 3 pounds?"
"Would you be willing to go without sugar for 10 minutes?"
"Would you be willing to help me write it *poorly*."
(for the Perfectionist)
"Would you be willing to do this until March...then we can renegotiate."

6. GET CREATIVE.

When you find out what the "very good reason" is behind an internal director's motivation (i.e. having weight on as a protection from appearing attractive or fighting a return of cancer or whatever)...when you find out what that is, get creative.

ONE CARDINAL RULE: Do not attempt to talk this person into another way of thinking, feeling or believing. This is an incredible waste of time, effort, energy and besides, it's insulting. Accept what they say, no matter how illogical it may seem to you.

(Trying to talk anybody out of how they feel is insulting. Saying things like, "Don't feel that way," will only escalate a problem. Instead, acknowledge it. Then work with that.)
Examples:
"I discovered that the reason I have the weight on is to drive my wife away--this is insane! She says it's not attractive and what I'm saying back to her is that there are things about *her* that I don't think are attractive. This is a stupid way of handling this problem."
"I discovered that the reason I don't pay my bills on time comes from a need to rebel. The only person being hurt by this is me!"
"I discovered that the reason I couldn't finish the story is because I was afraid of what my mother would think if she ever read it."
"I discovered that the reason that I live in an old house is because I believe that people who live in old houses *don't move*. I'm sick of moving so I bought an old house."
"I discovered that the reason I wouldn't let myself own a new Jaguar isn't because I couldn't afford it but because I

didn't want to distance myself from my lower income parents and relatives."

"I discovered that the reason I couldn't be thin is because I would lose my friends who also can't seem to lose weight."

(These may all appear to you to be ridiculous, illogical reasons. That's a judgement call on your part. Leave your judgements out of this because the communication won't work if you're passing judgements all the time. Instead...)

Ask yourself, how can I take care of this "very good reason" in *another way?* How can I give myself the same level of protection, but in another way?

Contemplating going into business for yourself? You might ask--what would have to be in place for me to feel comfortable starting my own business? How much money would I have to have in the bank before I could feel secure going on my own? Would the kids have to be finished with college first?

Your internal directors know EXACTLY what would have to be in place before it would be OK for you to start your own business. If you ask them, they will tell you. Write it down. It may be a terribly far-fetched list but at least you will know what it is.

Writers block? Frequently, perfectionism is the barracade to watching the words flow. Don't try to get it right, get it written. Only one cause of writers block-- FEAR. Any commitment to something that results in growth will scare you.

Don't ask: "How can I stop being afraid?"
Instead, ask: "Am I willing to be afraid for awhile?"
It's either...
  "I don't want to write."
  "I don't know what to write."
   or
  "I want it to be perfect."
Write to your protecting mechanism. "Thank you for helping me and trying to protect me. Now, would you be willing to...
  ...talk it into a recorder?"
  ...design the cover of the book?"
  ...list who would want it?"
  ...do research?"
  ...whatever...

7. Agree to renegotiate.

Your chances of influencing yourself (getting weight off and keeping it off, gaining financial independence and staying that way) will escalate dramatically when you promise your internal director-in-charge that, at a future time, you agree to update and examine how things are going and that you are open to renegotiate.

If you lose 60 pounds and your life turns into a giant mess and you truly believe that your new slender form is the reason, *and you just can't handle it,* then you'd better go have another conversation. FAST.

If your career takes off like a rocket, leaving your spouse frightened and confused, your family life in shambles, probably time to have additional conversations in your Internal Theatre.

Your internal directors will work for you if they feel that you really will listen and be open to renegotiate in the future.

Example: (to the Internal Fat Person)

"Would you be willing to take the weight off until March? At that time, I promise, that if my life has gotten weird and I can't handle it any other way, we can put the weight back on."

OR

"Would you be willing to have things be weird for awhile, while I experience being thin?

(to the Internal People Pleaser/Nice Guy)

"Would you be willing to be uncomfortable while I work on my assertiveness skills and my self-confidence?"

(to the Internal Social Director)

"Would you be willing to postpone getting together with friends until I get three chapters of my book written?"

Got the idea?

You will never meet more fascinating people than the people who are on the inside of your head. Television will be boring compared to the conversations you'll have.

Go with an Attitude of Gratitude: always thanking the characters for communicating with you! They have the power, otherwise you wouldn't be reading this, so bring a lot of respect with you--they deserve it.

TIPS & SECRETS FOR INNER THEATRE SUCCESS:

Objectify it. Write: what benefits might a person get from this behavior? What pay value (no matter how wild--be creative--be outrageous--be imaginative--be illogical) might an unusual person get from this behavior?

Ask: **"What am I pretending not to know?"**

Ask: "What would a person need to do in order to get past this?"

Ask: "If _____ (fill in a name...like, say, General George Patton or Miss Piggy or Sherlock Holmes) had this problem, what would they do? When you're finished laughing over that one, right down the solution.

Once you've brainstormed a list of possible things to do...

Ask: Is there anything on this list I'd be willing to do *today*--or for the next hour? for the next 5 minutes?

One day at a time. Sometimes one *minute* at a time. One pound at a time. One page at a time. Think about it. All you have to do is write one page. All you have to do is lose *one* pound!

You don't have to lose 35 pounds...or 60 pounds...or 10 pounds. You only have to lose ONE.

You don't have to write an entire book. You don't have to write 250 pages or 110 pages. Just ONE page. Just ONE word. Just ONE letter.

Ask yourself: "What will happen if I'm successful?"

At being thin. At having money. At writing. At being creative. At being a success.

Vividly imagine it. In detail. You are as _____ as you want to be (rich, thin, etc.)...now, how is your life different?

If you succeed, what person or persons in your life *wouldn't like it?* If you got what you wanted, you might be alienated in some form. What does that look like to you?

What's the worst that would happen?

Big question: Are you willing *right now* to live with that?

Pete discovered that he would lose a large portion of how he described himself, how he saw himself, if he quit drinking.

Gregarious Bill was successful with his 70 pound weight loss until he walked into a room and no one recognized him. Always the darling in any crowd, he felt left out and not willing to feel alienated, gained the weight back.

Jane sacrified sunny days and many lunches with friends to get her writing finished and published, only to discover none of her friends had enough winning spirits of their own to accept her success. Jane developed new contacts and new friends that could accept it.

Pamela knew full well, once she really, *really* imagined herself thin, that her husband would never be able to handle it. She decided to lose the weight anyway, watched and listened as he made every effort to sabotage her efforts, did what she could in couples' counselling and after she took off 100 pounds, she willingly lost another 160 pounds (her husband).

David discovered that if he didn't procrastinate on his taxes he wouldn't be the center of attention every April with the family. Tax paying can be the source of much drama in a household and David relished the starring role.

Remember that, in all their misery, people are getting what they want. And if they complain about it, it's giving them something to complain about, something to talk about. People get what they want. The mystery is figuring out what it is that you really, really want. Somebody on the inside wants it...and they want it for a very good reason. You job is to discover the reason and then give yourself that benefit *without the use of the sabotage.*

Allison had called it quits with her married lover six times in the past six weeks. The drama of it all was beginning to bore even Allison who had a great capacity for enduring it. She didn't want to be the Other Woman but she didn't want to lose her "Nice Guy" badge with her lover in the process. Many of us, in an effort to be Nice Guys or Good Sports, sacrifice an inner goal. On what seemed to be a whim, Allison posed as a nude model for an all-female art class. When she proudly displayed one of the sketches to her paramour, he was outraged and stormed out of her life permanently. Allison felt an unusual sense of relief as he drove away, a feeling she hadn't anticipated. It took a couple of hours before she realized that unconsciously she had created this situation and that someone deep inside her had masterminded it. Allison, consciously unable to find the courage, had tried "reasoning" with herself. Obviously one of her internal directors decided for her and solved her problem.

Even Allison could find the humor in a man who considered her posing nude for an art class as more immoral than adultery.

WHEN YOU NEED TO GET UNSTUCK...

On paper, answer the following questions:
I have now come to the end of my life and I'm really disappointed that I didn't...

_____
_____
_____
_____
_____

I have come to the end of my life and I'm really *glad* that I:

_____
_____
_____
_____
_____

HEAD-ON-THE-PILLOW TEST

As you put your head down on your pillow tonight, ask yourself this question:
"I just traded 24 hours for what I got today. Am I happy with the trade?"

ONE GREAT TRUTH OF BUSINESS

God can't drive a parked car.
Do *something* and something else will happen.

AFFIRMATIONS

Kinda fun and you don't even have to believe in 'em to have 'em work!
Some favorites:
I have time and I'm ready for more.
I have health and I'm ready for more.
I have money and I'm ready for more.
I have chutzpah and I'm ready for more.
I have humor and I'm ready for more.
I have insight and I'm ready for more.
I have discipline and I'm ready for more.
I have strength and I'm ready for more.
I have compassion and I'm ready for more.
I have _____ and I'm ready for more.
    (fill in what you need today)
I believe that something good is going to happen to me.
This day is the door that opens to my greatest year.
I am pleased and grateful for the progress I have made.
I give thanks that I have within me everything needed
    for success.
I rest and relax, certain that my life is under the direction
    of my good heart.
I am at peace with the past, forgiving myself and all others.
There is enough. What I am doing is enough.
Money finds me and I rejoice when it arrives.
I give generously and receive abundantly.
My life moves at a comfortable pace.
I am a success.
I deserve to be a success.
I chose to be a success.
Every day and every way I am getting healthier and healthier, happier and happier, thinner and thinner, richer and richer.

Additional Help (books/tapes/videos):

WRITE YOURSELF THIN by Toni Lynn Allawatt
   CompCare Publishers
   2415 Annapolis Lane
   Minneapolis, Minnesota
   1-800-328-3330

Alyce's FAT CHANCE
   by Alyce Cornyn-Selby
   Beynch Press Publishing Co.
   1928 S. E. Ladd Avenue
   Portland, Oregon 97214
   Phone orders: *Zelda* 1-800-937-7771

WISHCRAFT: How To Get What You Really Want
   by Barbara Sher
   Ballatine
   212-222-6973

SELF-SABOTAGE Audiocassette
   by Alyce Cornyn-Selby
   Beynch Press Publishing Co.
   1928 S. E. Ladd Avenue
   Portland, Oregon 97214
   Phone orders: *Zelda* 1-800-937-7771

MILITARY BRATS
   by Mary Edwards Wertsch
   Harmony Books
   201 E. 50 Street
   NY NY 10022

Also recommended is the Ira Progoff Intensive Journal Course taught at many colleges and universities.

QUOTES

I'd rather fail doing something I love than be a success doing something I hate.
  --George Burns

I've been absolutely terrified every moment of my life and I've never let it keep me from doing a single thing that I wanted to do.
  --Georgia O'Keeffe

Success IS all it's cracked up to be. Life gets better, the work is nicer, and I'm nicer.
  --Daniel J. Travanti

Success does not depend on how you *feel*.
  --Barbara Sher

The way to succeed is to double your failure rate.
  --Thomas J. Watson

This is your *Life;* it's not a dress rehearsal!
  --Cher

The greenhorn is the ultimate victor of all adventures.
  --Oscar Wilde

They never erected a statue to those who let well enough alone.
  --Anonymous

Go out on a limb--that's where the fruit is!
  --Unknown

In great attempts, it is glorious even to fail.
  --Anonymous

It's not what happens to me but how I handle it that determines my well being.
  --Dick Anderson

ORDER FORM

"Alyce is a thorough researcher and an unconventional thinker. Her books reflect these contrasts."
--*In Unison Magazine*

BOOKS

Quantity		Title	
	$7.95 each	Alyce's FAT CHANCE	
	$7.95 each	Teamwork & Team Sabotage	
	$7.95 each	Why Winners Win	
	$7.95 each	Take Your Hands Off My Attitude!	
	$7.95 each	I Don't Have To & You Can't Make Me!	
	$11.95 each	Procrastinator's Success Kit	
	$11.95 each	Did She Leave Me Any Money?	

TAPES

Quantity		Title	
	$9.95 each	I Used To Be Fat	
	$9.95 each	Teamwork	
	$9.95 each	Why Winners Win	
	$7.95 each	SONGS	
	$9.95 each	Self-Sabotage	

VIDEO

Quantity		Title	
	$79. each	"VIDEO: Alyce"	
	TIMES Newspaper ★		
	$1.25 each OR FREE with $15 purchase		

Total for Products:_____
★ Shipping, $2 per item:_____
On prepaid MAIL-IN Orders (ONLY) over $35, shipping is free.

____Yes, please have Alyce autograph my personal copy.
____Yes, please send "I Need a Good Speaker" brochure.

Checks payable: **BEYNCH PRESS**, 1928 S. E. Ladd Ave., Portland, OR 97214

Name:_ _

Address:_ _ _ _ _ _ _ _ _ _ _ _ _ _ _ _ _ _ _ _

City:_ _ _ _ _ _ _ _ _ _ State:_ _ _ _ Zip:_ _ _ _ _

For Credit Card or Phone Orders: 1-800-937-7771
Note: Different shipping rates apply for phone orders...ask for details.